AURA GARDEN GUIDES

Nicholas Hall

Clematis & Climbing Plants

AURA BOOKS

Aura Garden Guides

Clematis &
Climbing Plants

Nicholas Hall

© 1996 Advanced Marketing (UK) Ltd.,
Bicester, England

Produced by:
Transedition Limited for
Aura Books, Bicester
and first published in 2002

Editing by:
Asgard Publishing Services, Leeds

Typesetting by:
Organ Graphic, Abingdon

Picture Credits
All photographs by the author
except as follows:
Maurice Bracher 7, 8bl, 18, 24b,
27tl, 32b, 34, 35, 38, 39, 40, 41,
44, 45, 48, 52bl, 54, 54–55, 55,
62, 66, 70, 71, 72, 77bl, 83bl, 91b,
95bl; Photos Horticultural 42, 47,
65, 67, 68

10 9 8 7
Printed in Dubai

ISBN 1 901683 14 1

Nicholas Hall's special interest and
expertise in the field of clematis and
climbers is reflected in the many
years he spent working with the
Worcestershire-based company
Treasures of Tenbury — owners of
the world-famous gardens of Burford
House, which also include the
National Collection of Clematis.
Before that he worked for a variety of
specialist nurseries, and since leaving
Burford House he has been involved
in setting up a training centre for
dyslexic people of all ages.

CONTENTS

Clematis *'Hagley Hybrid'*

The world of climbers

The term 'climbing plant' covers a multitude of very different kinds of plants, ranging from the familiar climbing rose to the exotic *Lapageria rosea*. Between these two extremes is the clematis — much loved and yet so often misunderstood.

Such plants have been cultivated for many centuries, and for a variety of reasons. The Virginia creeper (*Parthenocissus quinquefolia*), for example, was used to cover an unsightly wall, or to add an air of romance and nostalgia. The rose around the cottage door was usually 'Mme Alfred Carrière' — a virtually thornless variety, its flowers beautifully perfumed and white with a flush of pink.

Climbing plants evolved to take advantage of the taller plants growing around them. They needed to reach the light in order to survive, so they adapted themselves by making use of neighbouring plants, using them as supports up which to grow. Once they had reached the light, they could then flower and eventually set seed to complete the cycle.

Climbers have evolved in various ways in order to achieve this end. The golden hop (*Humulus lupulus* 'Aureus') and wisteria twine themselves around a host plant. Ivies (*Hedera* spp.) and Virginia creeper (*Parthenocissus quinquefolia*) have small pads that stick to plants or walls, while plants like the clematis use their leaf stem to attach themselves. The most aggressive method is found among the roses — vigorous climbers such as *Rosa filipes* 'Kiftsgate' use their viciously downward-pointing spines to attach themselves to even the tallest trees.

The different ways in which climbers grow, each with the same objective of finding the sunlight, are of interest in themselves. But they also give us an indication of where to grow these plants and how to grow them. Climbers are among the most adaptable of plants, and among the most rewarding to grow.

Lapageria rosea *looks really exotic with its magnificent flowers and leathery leaves.*

The montanas are noted for their vigour — this specimen of Clematis montana *'Rubens' has colonised a* tree.

The clematis

Clematis has been grown in this country for centuries, but the only native species is *Clematis vitalba* or old man's beard. Its common name stems from the masses of fluffy seed heads that it produces in the autumn. According to various herbals, the stems were also smoked by shepherds and gypsies — hence its local name shepherd's bacca.

Late in the 16th century *Clematis viticella* and *C. integrifolia* were introduced into Britain from Europe. These were followed in quick succession by *C. cirrhosa*, *C. flammula* and the herbaceous *C. recta*.

One or two species came over from newly opened parts of America in the 17th century, but the most exciting introduction arrived from China around 1776. This was a form of *Clematis florida* with double greenish-white flowers. It was probably the variety now grown under the name *C. florida* 'Flore Pleno'. This plant's sister *C. florida* 'Sieboldii' followed in 1836, together with two other Chinese species, *C. patens* and *C. lanuginosa*.

The decades that followed saw an explosion in the number of plants introduced. Hardly a year passed without the appearance of some new and exciting variety, usually from China or the Far East.

The first recorded clematis cross was carried out by a Mr Henderson, and was between *Clematis integrifolia* and *C. viticella*. This resulted in the hybrid *C.* × *eriostemon*, which is still available today.

The biggest advances in clematis breeding were with the three original Chinese species, *Clematis florida*, *C. patens* and *C. lanuginosa*, which are jointly responsible for all the large-flowered hybrids that we grow today. *C. florida* crossed with *C. patens* or *C. lanuginosa* produced the double hybrids. *C. patens* was responsible for the large-flowered forms that bloom early in the year but only once. *C. lanuginosa* gave us the so-called twice-flowering forms, which flower early on old wood and again later on the new shoots. *C.* 'Nelly Moser' is a classic example of the latter.

In the late 19th century clematis hybrids were being introduced at a gallop. New cultivars, usually bearing the name of some member of the nobility, were offered to an eager public with ever-increasing frequency from nurseries all over Europe.

Clematis florida *'Sieboldii' was introduced from China in 1836.*

Clematis viticella 'Etoile Violette', seen here growing through a conifer

Huge displays were created, and clematis were so popular that they were even being used as bedding plants. All went well until the turn of the century, when the clematis suddenly went out of fashion.

This slump in popularity is usually attributed to the onset of the clematis wilt disease, which first made its appearance at about this time. This certainly would not have helped, but one cannot help wondering whether the sheer number of varieties, many of them very similar in appearance, did not make the task of choosing between them so tiresome that people moved on to other things. This is a danger that we could easily be facing again. How many different types of *Clematis tangutica, C. montana* or *C.* 'Nelly Moser' do we need before we finally give up trying to decide which one to grow?

However, with the advent of good-quality colour printing, and more importantly colour television, clematis have started to regain their popularity. There is nothing quite like a well-grown clematis for providing a 'photo opportunity'. Gardeners and nurserymen have started to show and use these plants more adventurously, so that clematis have at last regained their rightful place as one of the most decorative and useful of garden plants.

The clematis flower

Clematis is the common name given to members of the plant genus *Clematis*, which in turn belongs to the family Ranunculaceae. This family also includes garden flowers such as anemones and delphiniums, with the buttercup as a native example.

The word 'clematis' is derived from the Greek word *klema* meaning a vine-branch, reflecting the way the plant grows and clings to its support.

The clematis flower is very unusual in that it has no petals. The sepals, which in other plants cover the emerging flower, have evolved to take the place of petals, and it is these that make the flower so colourful. Sometimes, as with the double varieties, some of

Above: Clematis alpina *'Frances Rivis'*

Left: Clematis tangutica, *showing both the yellow flowers and the seed heads*

Terms used in classification

Note the way plant names are given within each category. The use of italics, inverted commas etc. indicates whether the plant is a species, a variety, a cultivar or whatever.

Species: This consists of closely related plants of a single kind, distinguished from other species by definable characteristics. Example: *Clematis viticella*.

Subspecies: A natural subgroup within a species. Example: *Clematis cirrhosa balearica*.

Variety: Small differences occur naturally within a species — perhaps a slight change of colour or leaf shape. Plants sharing such a characteristic are classed as a variety. Example: *Clematis fargesii* var. *souleii*.

Hybrid: When two different species or varieties are deliberately crossed, the resulting offspring are known as hybrids. Example: *Clematis* × *eriostemon*.

Cultivar: This is an abbreviation of 'cultivated variety', and is sometimes loosely termed 'variety'. Cultivars are the result of deliberate crossing under cultivation of a species and a hybrid, two hybrids, or perhaps even one of these with another cultivar. Most cultivated forms of clematis fall under this heading. Example: *Clematis* 'Daniel Deronda'.

the stamens have also taken on the appearance of petals.

The size of the flower varies enormously, from a myriad of tiny stars to the large flowers produced by certain hybrids, which under the right conditions can grow as large as a dinner plate.

The stamens, or male parts of the flower, can also be brightly coloured, varying from bright gold to a muddy brown. They are a useful means of identifying different cultivars within the same colour range.

After pollination, the female part of the flower swells to form a seed head. Each ripe seed head has a fluffy tail that is carried on the wind, enabling the plant to disperse its progeny. On some species, notably *Clematis tangutica*, the seed heads are beautiful in themselves, providing yet another source of pleasure that may continue for many months.

These magnificent blooms belong to Clematis 'Richard Pennell'.

Clematis types

Clematis hirsutissima *var.* scottii *is noted for its tiny flowers.*

The categories used below are designed so as to give you an overview of the different types of clematis available and the various ways in which they can be used to best effect in the garden.

Clematis have been grouped in many different ways in the past; at one time no fewer than ten categories were used by a single company. We have attempted to simplify the system so as to reflect those criteria that are most useful for gardening purposes, such as the flowering times, the manner of growth and the consequent pruning requirements of each plant.

Among the early large-flowered hybrids, the twice-flowering forms have not been separated from their relatives that flower only once. This is because their pruning requirements are the same, as are the various ways in which they can be used.

The genus *Clematis* must surely be one of the most diverse among the flowering plants, ranging from the tiny *C. hirsutissima* var. *scottii* to romping great thugs such as *C. rehderiana*. Between these two extremes we find a whole host of exotic large-flowered hybrids, both double and single. This diversity is one aspect that makes clematis such rewarding plants, offering so many different possibilities for gardeners to develop and experiment with new ideas.

Evergreen clematis

These plants are among the most popular forms of clematis.

A selection of evergreen clematis (no pruning required)

Species or cultivar	Flowers	Position	Flowering time	Growth height
Clematis armandii	small, white	sheltered	Mar.–Apr.	30 ft (9 m)
C. armandii 'Snowdrift'	white, larger than species	sheltered	Mar.–Apr.	15 ft (5 m)
C. a. 'Apple Blossom'	small, white, pink in bud	sheltered	Mar.–Apr.	30 ft (9 m)
C. cirrhosa	small, cream, brown speckles	sunny	Jan.–Mar.	20 ft (6 m)
C. c. balearica	small, cream, red speckles	sunny	Jan.–Mar.	20 ft (6 m)
C. c. 'Freckles'	small, cream, red inside	sunny	Jan.–Mar.	20 ft (6 m)
C. c. 'Wisley Cream'	small, pure cream	sunny	Jan.–Mar.	20 ft (6 m)

Unfortunately they are also responsible for some of the biggest disappointments.

The evergreens can be divided into two distinct groups according to the two original species, *Clematis armandii* and *C. cirrhosa* (still sometimes called *C. calycina*). The armandiis come from China, while the cirrhosas are from the Balearic Islands in the western Mediterranean. Although both groups are generally hardy, they do require some specialist treatment to give of their best.

Clematis armandii and its various cultivars have broad, leathery dark-green leaves that are particularly prone to damage from cold winds; the plant is left looking brown and tired. Because of this the armandiis are best planted in a sheltered position that also gets a fair amount of sun. This is essential so that the wood can ripen and the flower buds can develop for the next season's floral display. The flowers have a delicious scent of vanilla, which can waft across the garden on warm spring evenings. *C. armandii* can be raised from seed, but is very variable in the size of flower and the amount of perfume it produces. You can be more confident of success if you search out a named cultivar such as *C. a.* 'Snowdrift'.

The cirrhosas are a little more temperamental, not in their growth or hardiness (they are very vigorous and as

hardy as any other clematis), but in their ability to flower. They are often suggested as an ideal early-flowering plant — and indeed, given the right position and a climate that suits them, they can produce their cup-shaped speckled

Clematis armandii is an evergreen species that needs a sunny, sheltered position.

bells as early as January. The snag is that they need plenty of winter sunshine to give of their best. So they should

11

never be recommended for gardens in the more northerly counties — or at least not unless they enjoy an exceptional microclimate.

If properly looked after, both armandiis and cirrhosas will grow and thrive in common with other clematis. But especially after July or August, you should avoid feeding them with anything other than potash. Too much nitrogen late in the year can encourage soft growth with no time left for ripening before the winter frosts cut it back.

Montanas and alpinas

This group of clematis contains species and varieties that are among the first to flower,

ranging from the compact to the very vigorous in growth.

Clematis alpina is a European species distinguished by its profusion of bright-blue nodding, bell-like flowers that open in April, or as early as March in a sheltered position. Among the various cultivars that have been produced, one of the best is *C. a.* 'Frances Rivis'. This has much longer sepals than the species, with a wonderful light-blue colouring.

Clematis macropetala is a very similar species from China. It was introduced early this century, and differs from *C. alpina* in having double flowers. The predominant colour is again a rich blue. Among the various cultivars,

Clematis alpina *'Willy'*

C. macropetala 'Markhams Pink' is the best-known pink-flowering form.

Alpina, macropetala and montana varieties

Alpina cultivars (no pruning required)

Species or cultivar	Flowers	Position	Flowering time	Growth height
C. alpina 'Burford White'	small, white, bell-shaped	any aspect	Apr.–May	8 ft (2.5 m)
C. a. 'Columbine'	small, blue, bell-shaped	any aspect	Apr.	8 ft (2.5 m)
C. a. 'Constance'	ruby-red, bell-shaped	any aspect	Apr.	8 ft (2.5 m)
C. a. 'Frances Rivis'	small, mid-blue, bell-shaped	any aspect	April	8 ft (2.5 m)
C. a. 'Frankie'	deep blue, bell-shaped	any aspect	Apr.	8 ft (2.5 m)
C. a. 'Helsinburg'	small, blue, bell-shaped	any aspect	Apr.	8 ft (2.5 m)
C. a. 'Pamela Jackman'	small, mid-blue, bell-shaped	any aspect	Apr.	8 ft (2.5 m)
C. a. 'Rosy Pagoda'	rosy-pink, bell-shaped	any aspect	Mar.–Apr.	8 ft (2.5 m)
C. a. 'Ruby'	small, purple-pink, bell-shaped	any aspect	Apr.	8 ft (2.5 m)
C. a. 'White Columbine'	small, white, bell-shaped	any aspect	Apr.–May	8 ft (2.5 m)
C. a. 'White Moth'	small, double, white, bell-shaped	any aspect	Apr.	8 ft (2.5 m)
C. a. 'Willy'	small, pink, bell-shaped	any aspect	Apr.	8 ft (2.5 m)

Macropetala species and cultivars (no pruning required)

Species or cultivar	Flowers	Position	Flowering time	Growth height
C. macropetala	small, blue	any aspect	Apr.–May	12 ft (3.5 m)
C. m. 'Blue Moon'	double, blue, white flecks	any aspect	Mar.–Apr.	8 ft (2.5 m)
C. m. 'Lagoon'	semi-double, violet, blue	any aspect	Apr.–May	12 ft (3.5 m)
C. m. 'Maidwell Hall'	large, double, deep blue, bell-shaped	any aspect	Apr.–May	8 ft (2.5 m)
C. m. 'Markhams Pink'	small, pink	any aspect	Apr.–May	12 ft (3.5 m)
C. m. 'Orchid'	double, ruby-red, cream centre	any aspect	Apr.	8 ft (2.5 m)
C. m. 'Pink Pearl'	double, rosy-pink, bell-shaped	any aspect	Mar.–Apr.	8 ft (2.5 m)
C. m. 'Snowbird'	small, white	any aspect	Apr.	12 ft (3.5 m)
C. m. 'White Swan'	large, creamy-white	any aspect	Apr.–May	8–10 ft (2.5–3 m)

*Clematis montana 'Pink Perfection'
— a clematis that smells good as
well as looking good*

Alpinas and macropetalas grow to only 7-8 ft (2-2.5 m) in height. They produce their main crop of flowers in early spring, with only a few sporadic blooms appearing in late summer. However, the display of seed heads after flowering provides a bonus, extending the period of interest into the

13

Clematis macropetala *belongs to the same group as the alpinas.*

late spring. The ferny light-green foliage is an added attraction.

Both the species and their hybrids and cultivars will grow happily in any position. They are totally hardy. If grown in a cold position and not overfed, they will tend to produce deeper-coloured flowers.

Montana species and cultivars (no pruning required)

Species or cultivar	Flowers	Position	Flowering time	Growth height
C. montana	small, white, in profusion	any aspect	Apr.–May	30 ft (9 m)
C. m. 'Elizabeth'	small, soft pink, scented	any aspect	May–Jun.	30 ft (9 m)
C. m. 'Freda'	cherry-pink with dark edges	any aspect	May–Jun.	30 ft (9 m)
C. m. 'Grandiflora'	small, white, scented	any aspect	May–Jun.	30 ft (9 m)
C. m. 'Pictons Variety'	small, deep satin-pink	any aspect	May–Jun.	20 ft (6 m)
C. m. 'Pink Perfection'	small, pink, scented	any aspect	May	30 ft (9 m)
C. m. 'Rubens'	small, pale mauve	any aspect	May–Jun.	30 ft (9 m)
C. m. 'Tetrarose'	small, deep rosy-mauve	any aspect	May–Jun.	30 ft (9 m)
C. m. 'Vera'	small, pink, scented	any aspect	May	30 ft (9 m)
C. m. 'Wilsonii'	small, white	any aspect	Jun.	30 ft (9 m)

Opposite: Clematis montana
'Pictons Variety' growing through a
conifer
Above: Clematis montana *'Rubens'*

Montanas

The montana group of clematis, unlike the alpinas, are well
known for their vigour, creating a profusion of star-like
flowers in the early spring.

Depending on the variety, they
will grow to heights of up to
50 ft (15 m), and are most
suitable for growing up quite
large trees.

One of the major benefits to
be obtained from growing
light-pink or white-flowered
montanas is the scent they
produce on a warm spring day.
Unfortunately, the darker-pink

varieties and the allied species
do not possess this characteristic. But species like *Clematis
vedrariensis* have attractive
foliage, which prolongs the
period of interest.

Like the alpinas, the montanas flower in April–May, and
will grow happily in a variety of
situations; they will even
tolerate quite deep shade.

Other similar species and cultivars (no pruning required)

Species or cultivar	Flowers	Position	Flowering time	Growth height
C. chrysocoma	small, white	best sheltered	May	20 ft (6 m)
C. c. 'Hybrid'	small, sugar-pink, in profusion	any aspect	Apr.–May	30 ft (9 m)
C. vedrariensis	medium, rosy/mauve	any aspect	May–Jun.	20 ft (6 m)
C. v. 'Hidcote'	small, deep pink	any aspect	May–Jun.	20 ft (6 m)
C. v. 'Highdown'	small, pink	any aspect	May–Jun.	20 ft (6 m)

Early large-flowered clematis

This group produces some of the largest flowers to be seen in the garden. If you look after them properly, cultivars such as the well-known *C.* 'Nelly Moser' will produce a vast array of plate-sized flowers in early summer.

However, like all prima donnas they have to be carefully nurtured to create the full

Right: Clematis *'King Edward VII' against a background of heathers*

Below: *The flowers of* Clematis *'Marie Boisselot' are large but delicate.*

A selection of early large-flowered clematis (light pruning required)

Cultivar	Flowers	Position	Flowering time	Growth height
C. 'Barbara Dibley'	large, petunia-red	sunny	May–Jun.; Aug.	10 ft (3 m)
C. 'Barbara Jackman'	large, blue with petunia bar	light shade	May–Jun.	10 ft (3 m)
C. 'Beauty of Richmond'	large, pale lavender	any aspect	Jun.–Aug.	10 ft (3 m)
C. 'Bees Jubilee'	large, deep-pink with rose bar	shady	May–Jun.; Aug.	10 ft (3 m)
C. 'Carnaby'	medium, deep pink	shady	May–Jun.	6 ft (2 m)
C. 'Corona'	large, purple-pink	sunny	May–Jun.; Aug.	8 ft (2.5 m)
C. 'Crimson King'	large, crimson`	sunny	Jun.–Sep.	12 ft (3.5 m)
C. 'Dawn'	large, pearly-pink	shady	May–Jun.; Aug.	10 ft (3 m)
C. 'Etoile de Malicorne'	lilac with magenta bar	any aspect	Jun.–Aug.	20 ft (6 m)
C. 'Etoile de Paris'	large, blue/mauve	any aspect	May–Jun.	10 ft (3 m)
C. 'Fair Rosamund'	large, white with pink bar, scented	any aspect	May–Jun.	12 ft (3.5 m)
C. 'Gillian Blades'	large, white with faint mauve edge	any aspect	May–Jun.; Sep.	12 ft (3.5 m)
C. 'H. F. Young'	large, wedgwood blue	any aspect	May–Jun.	10 ft (3 m)
C. 'Joan Picton'	large, lilac with lighter bar	any aspect	May–Jun.; Sep.	10 ft (3 m)
C. 'Kathleen Dunford'	large, deep lavender	sunny	Jun.–Jul; Aug.	12 ft (3.5 m)
C. 'King Edward VII'	large, pale violet with crimson bar	shady	Jun.–Aug.	10 ft (3 m)
C. 'Lady Londesborough'	medium, pale mauve	any aspect	May–Jun.	10 ft (3 m)
C. 'Lasurstern'	large, blue	any aspect	May–Jun.; Sep.	12 ft (3.5 m)
C. 'Lincoln Star'	large, raspberry-pink	shady	May–Jun.	12 ft (3.5 m)
C. 'Marie Boisselot'	large, white	any aspect	Jun.–Sep.	10 ft (3 m)
C. 'Miss Bateman'	medium, creamy-white	any aspect	May–Jun.	8 ft (2.5 m)
C. 'Moonlight'	large, creamy-yellow	shady	May–Jun.	10 ft (3 m)
C. 'Nelly Moser'	large, mauve with lilac bar	shady	May–Jun.; Aug.–Sep.	10 ft (3 m)
C. 'Niobe'	large, deep red	any aspect	Jun.–Jul.; Aug.	10 ft (3 m)
C. 'Richard Pennell'	large, deep purple	any aspect	May–Jul.	12 ft (3.5 m)
C. 'Vino'	large, wine-red	any aspect	May–Jun.	10 ft (3 m)
C. 'Wadas Primrose'	large, creamy-white	ideal for shade	May–Jun.	10 ft (3 m)
C. 'Warsaw Nike'	royal purple with gold centre	sunny	Jun.–Sep.	8–12 ft (2.5–3.5 m)
C. 'Will Goodwin'	large, lavender	any aspect	Jun.–Sep.	12 ft (3.5 m)

effect. All too often you will see poor Nelly strung up against a furiously hot wall, turning a gentle shade of grey above the yellowing leaves. Lots of water and potash are what's required for Nelly and her ilk to thrive. They will need about 7 gallons (over 30 litres) of water per week throughout the summer months, adding some tomato fertiliser every fortnight or so.

Clematis 'Crimson King'

Several cultivars in this group are particularly rewarding in that they flower twice in the season. The first profusion of flowers appears in May or June, lasting several weeks. A lull during the main growth period is followed by yet another flowering in August, which is less abundant but just as rewarding.

Many of these varieties also produce fat seed heads after flowering. These are quite attractive, and can either be retained on the plant or used for indoor decoration. Leaving them on the plant will not

18

Above: Clematis *'Bees Jubilee' likes plenty of shade.*

have any adverse effect, and they can be snipped off later when they have served their purpose.

This group includes a variety or cultivar to suit almost every position in the garden. However, because of the size of the flowers, it's best to find somewhere sheltered from the worst affects of any summer storms. The flowers are large but delicate, and their big surface area means they can be easily shredded by summer storms unless some protection is provided. On they other hand, all these plants are hardy enough to withstand the rigours of most English winters without any ill effects.

Double and semi-double varieties

These clematis are among the most exotic of all climbing plants to be found in the garden. They range from the almost peony-like blooms of *Clematis* 'Proteus' to the delicate yet abundant *C. viticella* 'Purpurea Plena Elegans'.

Often you may purchase a double variety from a nursery or garden centre, take it home and plant it, and almost immediately a flower bud will appear only to open as a single flower. This is perfectly normal, and nine times out of ten there is nothing amiss. The reason is that the double varieties (with the exception of *Clematis viticella* 'Purpurea Plena Elegans') produce their double flowers only in May and June on the previous year's growth; they will flower again later in the summer, but this time they only produce single flowers. It follows that newly purchased plants will

Clematis *'Proteus'*

have not had the time to produce enough wood for double flowers to develop.

To give of their best, these clematis require the same cultural treatment as the early large-flowered varieties. But they are best planted in a sunny position, where the summer sun will ripen the current growth to provide next year's crop of flowers.

Sometimes a double white variety such as *Clematis* 'Duchess of Edinburgh' will produce green outer sepals. This effect will become even more pronounced if the variety is planted in a shady position, where the entire flower can become green — a pheno-menon much beloved of flower arrangers.

Clematis *'Vyvyan Pennell' produces double flowers initially ...*

A selection of double and semi-double varieties (light pruning required)

Cultivar	Flowers	Position	Flowering time	Growth height
C. 'Beauty of Worcester'	large, deep blue, double	sunny	May–Jul.	10 ft (3 m)
C. 'Countess of Lovelace'	large, lilac/blue, double	sunny	May–Jul.	10 ft (3 m)
C. 'Daniel Deronda'	large, purple/blue, double	sunny	May–Aug.	10 ft (3 m)
C. 'Duchess of Edinburgh'	medium, white, double	sunny	Jun.–Aug.	10 ft (3 m)
C. 'Jackmanii Alba'	white, double, later single	any aspect	Jun.–Sep.	12 ft (3.5 m)
C. 'Kathleen Dunford'	large, deep lavender	sunny	Jun.–Jul.; Aug.	12 ft (3.5 m)
C. 'Lady Caroline Nevill'	large, blue/mauve, semi-double	sunny	May–Jun.; Aug.	20 ft (6 m)
C. 'Mrs George Jackman'	large, cream/white, double, later single	any aspect	May–Sep.	10 ft (3 m)
C. 'Proteus'	large, mauve, double, later single	shade/semi-shade	May–Jun.; Aug.	10 ft (3 m)
C. 'Royalty'	large, plum-purple, double in May	any aspect	May; Aug.	10 ft (3 m)
C. 'Sylvia Denny'	medium, white, double, later single	any aspect	May–Jun.	10 ft (3 m)
C. 'Vyvyan Pennell'	large, lavender, double, later single	any aspect	May–Aug.	10 ft (3 m)
C. 'Walter Pennell'	large, deep lilac with carmine bar	any aspect	May–Jun.	12 ft (3.5 m)

... followed by singles later in the season.

summer. The flowers hang well away from the plant, making it an ideal subject for growing up a light-coloured conifer. For despite being double, *C. v.* 'Purpurea Plena Elegans' can be treated just like any other viticella: you can cut it back quite hard in the autumn, allowing the host plant to take pride of place before the final prune in February.

Below: *The double flowers of Clematis 'Jackmanii Alba' also give way to singles later on.*

Many of these varieties are compact in growth. These are especially suited to growing in containers, where their large, heavy blooms can be given protection from the worst of the weather.

The value of the single flowers should also not be underestimated. *Clematis* 'Duchess of Sutherland' is perhaps one of the finest late-flowering reds available, while *C.* 'Royalty's myriad of single flowers carry on almost until the first frost of autumn sends the plant into dormancy.

The one exception among the double varieties is *Clematis viticella* 'Purpurea Plena Elegans'. This vigorous plant will grow as much as 15 ft (4.5 m) in a single year, producing its small, perfectly formed double violet blooms into late

The superb carmine-red flowers of Clematis 'Ville de Lyon' — a favourite summer hybrid

Summer hybrids

These particular clematis share a number of advantages. Firstly, they flower at a time of year when other plants are past their best. More importantly, they flower on the current year's growth, which means they respond well to hard pruning each year.

There is only one drawback: by the time these plants have begun to flower, many if not all of the lower leaves have either yellowed or died, leaving the lower part bare and ugly. This makes the summer hybrids admirable subjects for growing through other trees and shrubs, where this unfortunate habit can be disguised by the host plant and only the growing and flowering portion remains visible.

The flower size of this group is less impressive than that of the early large-flowered forms. However, if you carry on feeding them with a high-potash fertiliser, the depth of colour can be markedly increased. You can also delay the flowering period somewhat by pruning extra hard and extra late — say, around March — which can provide a much-needed display of late-summer or early-autumn colour.

A selected list of summer hybrids

Cultivar	Flowers	Position	Pruning needed	Flowering time	Growth height
C. 'Ascotiensis'	large, blue	any aspect	hard	Jul.–Aug.	10 ft (3 m)
C. 'Comtesse de Bouchaud'	large, mauve/pink	any aspect	hard	Jul.–Aug.	10 ft (3 m)
C. 'Crimson King'	large, crimson	sunny	light	Jun.–Sep.	12 ft. (3.5 m)
C. 'Duchess of Sutherland'	large, carmine	any aspect	light	Jun.–Aug.	10 ft (3 m)
C. 'Gypsy Queen'	large, violet/purple	sunny	hard	Jul.–Aug.	12 ft (3.5 m)
C. 'Hagley Hybrid'	medium, rosy/mauve	any aspect	hard	Jun.–Aug.	8 ft (2.5 m)
C. 'Huldine'	medium, pearly/white	any aspect	hard	Jul.–Sep.	10 ft (3 m)
C. 'Jackmanii Superba'	large, dark purple	any aspect	hard	Jul.–Sep.	12 ft (3.5 m)
C. 'John Huxtable'	large, white	any aspect	hard	Jul.–Aug.	10 ft (3 m)
C. 'Kathleen Wheeler'	large, plum/mauve	any aspect	light	Jun.–Sep.	12 ft (3.5 m)
C. 'King George V'	flesh-pink with darker bar	shady	light	Jul.–Aug.	10 ft (3 m)
C. 'Lawsoniana'	large, mauve	any aspect	light	Jun.–Jul.; Aug.	15 ft (4.5 m)
C. 'Lilacina Floribunda'	large, rich purple	any aspect	hard	Jul.–Aug.; Sep.	15 ft (4.5 m)
C. 'Mme Edouard André'	medium, red	any aspect	hard	Jun.–Aug.	8 ft (2.5 m)
C. 'Mme Grangé'	large, red/purple	any aspect	hard	Jul.–Aug.	12 ft (3.5 m)
C. 'Mrs Hope'	large, light blue	semi-shade	light	Jul.–Aug.	12 ft (3.5 m)
C. 'Perle d'Azur'	medium, azure-blue	any aspect	hard	Jul.–Sep.	15 ft (4.5 m)
C. 'Prince Charles'	medium, blue	any aspect	hard	Jun.–Sep.	10 ft (3 m)
C. 'Prins Hendrick'	large, blue	sunny	hard	Jul.–Aug.	10 ft (3 m)
C. 'Ramona'	large, lavender	any aspect	light	Jul.–Sep.	20 ft (6 m)
C. 'Star of India'	medium, deep purple with carmine bar	any aspect	hard	Jul.–Aug.	12 ft (3.5 m)
C. 'Victoria'	medium, rosy mauve	any aspect	hard	Jul.–Aug.	12 ft (3.5 m)
C. 'Ville de Lyon'	large, carmine-red	any aspect	hard	Jun.–Sep.	20 ft (6 m)

Even though these clematis are not normally recommended for growing in containers, it is possible to create a successful combination of *Clematis* 'Comtesse de Bouchaud' and *C.* 'Lady Northcliffe'. If you first grow 'Comtesse de Bouchaud' up a tall structure, then allow the more compact 'Lady Northcliffe' to twine around the base, this can work extremely well over several years. 'Lady Northcliffe' only needs a light prune, while 'Comtesse de Bouchaud' should be pruned hard. The plants will stay in flower for months, and the combination of light-blue and pink blooms will prove most effective.

Left: Clematis *'Mme Grangé' probably flowers for longer than any other cultivar.*
Below: Clematis *'Jackmanii Superba' surrounded by dahlias*

A magnificent flower belonging to Clematis 'Lawsoniana' — its colour can be improved by the application of a high-potash fertiliser.

Below: Clematis *'Huldine'*

Clematis viticella and its hybrids

All the cultivars in this section stem from crosses with the European species *Clematis viticella*, which in late summer produces a massive profusion of pretty little mauve bells. This species has been in cultivation in this country since the 16th century, and is still very popular today.

Because of the parent species, all the cultivars flower very profusely, and all of them are in bloom through August and September. The colour range has become very diverse, ranging from the red of *Clematis viticella* 'Abundance' to the purple of *C. v.* 'Etoile Violette', with whites and pinks in between. There is also the only

25

A selection of viticella cultivars and hybrids (hard pruning required)

Species or cultivar	Flowers	Position	Flowering time	Growth height
Clematis viticella	small, mauve/purple	any aspect	Jul.–Sep.	15 ft (4.5 m)
C. v. 'Abundance'	small, red	any aspect	Jul.–Sep.	12 ft (3.5 m)
C. v. 'Alba Luxurians'	small, creamy-white	any aspect	Jul.–Sep.	10 ft (3 m)
C. v. 'Blue Belle'	blue/mauve	any aspect	Aug.–Sep.	10 ft (3 m)
C. v. 'Elvan'	small, lilac with white centre	any aspect	Aug.–Sep.	15 ft (4.5 m)
C. v. 'Etoile Violette'	medium, violet	any aspect	Jul.–Sep.	10 ft (3 m)
C. v. 'Kermesina'	small, red	any aspect	Jul.–Aug.	12 ft (3.5 m)
C. v. 'Krim'	pale violet, bell-shaped	any aspect	Aug.–Sep.	10 ft (3 m)
C. v. 'Little Nell'	small, white with mauve edge	any aspect.	Jul.–Sep.	12 ft (3.5 m)
C. v. 'Mme Julia Correvon'	small, wine-red	any aspect	Jul.–Aug.	12 ft (3.5 m)
C. v. 'Margot Koster'	small, rosy red, profuse	any aspect	Aug.–Sep	12 ft (3.5 m)
C. v. 'Minuet'	small, white with mauve edge	any aspect	Jul.–Aug.	12 ft (3.5 m)
C. v. 'Purpurea Plena Elegans'	small, double, purple	any aspect	Jul.–Sep.	12 ft (3.5 m)
C. v. 'Royal Velours'	small, deep purple	any aspect	Jul.–Sep.	12 ft (3.5 m)
C. v. 'Venosa Violacea'	medium, white with purple margins	any aspect	Jun.–Aug.	10 ft (3 m)

double variety to flower so late in the year — the unfortunately named *C. v.* 'Purpurea Plena Elegans'.

All these hybrids benefit from a hard pruning each year. Thanks to their general vigour and tenacity for life, they are ideal for growing through and up other trees and shrubs that flower earlier on, or combined with shrubs with ornamental foliage, where the combinations of colours can be extremely attractive.

The flowers of Clematis viticella 'Venosa Violacea' can be seen here peering through Caryopteris × clandonensis 'Worcester Gold'.

Clematis viticella 'Mme Julia Correvon'

which die down to a basal clump each year, and this is exactly what these clematis do. They can be treated like any other herbaceous plants, and can be lifted and divided in the autumn as required. They also need support — and while semi-herbaceous forms such as *Clematis × durandii* or *C. integrifolia* will happily clamber through other plants,

Below: *The flowers of* Clematis recta *are only small, but their scent is guaranteed to attract butterflies.*

Herbaceous clematis

It seems slightly odd that the first recorded clematis hybrid was a herbaceous one. It was named *Clematis × eriostemon*, and was the result of a cross between the two European species *C. integrifolia* and *C. viticella*. With its bright-blue bells it is still very much worth growing. Among the most eye-catching combinations that can be seen is a *C. × eriostemon* tumbling over a wall covered with a golden-foliaged ivy such as *Hedera helix* 'Gold Heart'.

The term 'herbaceous' is used to denote those plants

27

A selection of herbaceous and semi-herbaceous clematis (hard pruning required)

Species or cultivar	Flowers	Position	Flowering time	Growth height
Clematis × durandii	medium, indigo-blue	any aspect	Jun.–Sep.	8 ft (2.5 m)
C. × eriostemon 'Hendersonii'	small, indigo-blue	any aspect	Jul.–Sep.	12 ft (3.5 m)
C. heracleifolia 'Côte d'Azur'	small, light blue	any aspect	Aug.–Sep.	3 ft (1 m)
C. h. 'Davidiana'	small, light blue	any aspect	Aug.–Sep.	3 ft (1 m)
C. h. 'Mrs Robert Brydon'	small, off-white	any aspect	Aug.–Sep.	3 ft (1 m)
C. h. 'Stans'	small, pale blue	any aspect	Jul.–Aug.	3 ft (1 m)
C. h. 'Wyevale'	small, deep blue	any aspect	Aug.–Oct.	3 ft (1 m)
C. integrifolia	small, blue	any aspect	Jul.	5 ft (1.5 m)
C. i. 'Alba'	small, white	any aspect	Jul.	5 ft (1.5 m)
C. i. 'Budapest'	small, dark blue	any aspect	Jul.	5 ft (1.5 m)
C. i. 'Hendersonii'	small, dark blue	any aspect	Jul.	5 ft (1.5 m)
C. i. 'Olgae'	small, pale blue	any aspect	Jul.	5 ft (1.5 m)
C. i. 'Rosea'	small, pink	any aspect	Jun.	5 ft (1.5 m)
C. × jouiniana	small, lavender	any aspect	Aug.–Sep.	20 ft (6 m)
C. × j. 'Praecox'	small, lavender	any aspect	Jul.–Sep.	20 ft (6 m)
C. recta	small, white	any aspect	May–Jun.	3 ft (1 m)
C. r. 'Purpurea'	small, white	any aspect	May–Jun.	3 ft (1 m)

others such as *C. heracleifolia* or *C. recta* will need the assistance of pea sticks, or one of the many herbaceous plant supports now available.

These last two species and their varieties make big plants indeed. As they only bloom once, and for a short period at that, they are perhaps best avoided in a small garden. However, they do possess a good scent, which attracts a variety of insect life. Butterflies in particular love to feed on the nectar of *Clematis recta*, adding extra colour to a plant that is otherwise rather dull.

Clematis × durandii has gorgeous blooms, and will happily clamber through other plants.

The purple-leaved form is rather better, and is worth seeking out.

In common with all clematis, these herbaceous plants respond well to generous feeding and copious amounts of water. They can provide a useful addition to your mid-summer garden.

The texensis cultivars

Clematis texensis is an intriguing plant. The flower is bright red in the best forms, and its shape is that of a small tube. This species appears to be a rather spindly grower, yet in the latter part of the 19th century it formed the basis for a number of hybrids named after various members of the nobility. They were produced by a Woking-based nursery, so became known as the Woking-ensis hybrids. Alas, very few of them have survived to this day — but those hybrids that have

Clematis texensis *is the species from which all the red cultivars are derived.*

A selection of texensis cultivars (hard pruning required)

Species or cultivar	Flowers	Position	Flowering time
Clematis texensis	small, scarlet	any aspect	Aug.–Sep.
C. t. 'Duchess of Albany'	small, pink with a cherry bar	any aspect	Aug.–Sep.
C. t. 'Etoile Rose'	cherry-red, tulip-shaped	any aspect	Aug.
C. t. 'Gravetye Beauty'	small, ruby-red	any aspect	Aug.–Sep.
C. t. 'Ladybird Johnson'	deep wine-red	any aspect	Aug.–Sep.
C. t. 'Pagoda'	small, pink	any aspect	Aug.–Sep.
C. t. 'Princess of Wales'	deep pink, tubular	any aspect	Aug.–Sep.
C. t. 'Sir Trevor Lawrence'	small, deep carmine	any aspect	Aug.–Sep.

Clematis texensis *'Pagoda' growing over heathers*

survived, together with some of the modern cultivars, are some of the most stunning plants that you are likely to find anywhere.

Oddly enough, many of the modern forms continue the noble tradition. *Clematis texensis* 'Princess of Wales' and *C. t.* 'Ladybird Johnson' are amongst the finest. Produced by Barry Fretwell at his Peverill Nurseries, the 'Princess of Wales' is a wonderful deep pink that almost glows, while 'Ladybird Johnson' is a deep wine-red. Both these new forms deserve a place in even the smallest garden.

All the texensis cultivars are perfectly hardy. By their very nature, however, they tend not to climb, preferring to scramble through other shrubby plants, where their upturned tulip-shaped flowers are produced in abundance, adding a quite exotic touch to the late-summer borders.

The texensis are all moderately vigorous in growth, so are best planted together with a comparable host — perhaps one of the low-growing cotoneasters, or the silver-leaved berberis with the dreadful name of *Berberis dictyophylla approximata*. Both of these will provide the support the clematis requires without themselves becoming swamped and spoiled.

Experience suggests that these varieties dislike being planted in tubs or containers, which are prone to dry out. Under such conditions, and also in dry positions in the garden, these plants will soon develop mildew, which if left unchecked can soon defoliate and eventually kill the plant.

Other clematis species and their hybrids

The genus *Clematis* is represented in every continent. This means these plants can be grown in a variety of climates and soil types, ranging from the chalky to the very acid.

In general, clematis are climbing plants that use their leaf stems to attach themselves to their host plants. However, there are also herbaceous forms that die down to ground level each year — *Clematis heracleifolia* from China, for example. Then there are those such as the European species *C. viticella* that will happily scramble along the ground while still providing a good display of flowers.

The white flowers of Clematis fargesii *var.* souleii *can look very effective against a background of dark-green foliage.*

The fact that clematis are so diverse means that the range of flower shapes and colours available is also very extensive. China alone has given us the delicate yellow bells of *Clematis tangutica*, together with those large, exotic-looking blooms produced by crossing *C. florida* with *C. patens* and *C. lanuginosa*.

Australasia, with its unusual natural history, provides some fascinating curiosities. *Clematis marmoria* is a tiny, white-flowered species that is best treated as an alpine, while *C. afoliata* is remarkably unusual, having replaced its leaves with tendrils and looking very like a climbing rush.

Other clematis species and their hybrids

Species or cultivar	Flowers (and foliage)	Position	Pruning needed	Flowering time	Growth height
Clematis aethusifolia	small, creamy-yellow	any aspect	hard	Jul.–Aug.	20 ft (6 m)
C. afoliata	small, creamy-yellow	sheltered	none	Mar.–Apr.	10 ft (3 m)
C. campaniflora	small, blue-white	any aspect	light	Jul.–Aug.	10 ft (3 m)
C. crispa	small, purple	sunny	hard	Jul.–Aug.	8 ft (2.5 m)
C. fargesii var. *souleii*	medium, white	any aspect	hard	Jun.–Sep.	20 ft (6 m)
C. fasciulifolia	small, white (silver-striped foliage)	sheltered	none	Jul.–Aug.	20 ft (6 m)
C. finetiana	small, white	sheltered	none	Jun.	15 ft (4.5 m)
C. flammula	small, white	any aspect	hard	Aug.–Oct.	12 ft (3.5 m)
C. gentianoides	small, pink	sunny	hard	Jul.–Aug.	10 ft (3 m)
C. glauca	small, yellow	any aspect	hard	Aug.–Sep.	30 ft (9 m)
C. gouriana	small, pink/white	any aspect	hard	Jul.–Aug.	20 ft (6 m)
C. koreana	yellow, bell-shaped	any aspect	none	Jul.–Aug.	
C. maximowicziana	small, white	sunny	hard	Sep.–Oct.	12 ft (3.5 m)
C. nepalensis	small, creamy-yellow	sheltered	none	Nov.–Jan.	20 ft (6 m)
C. orientalis	orange/yellow, bell-shaped	shade/semi-shade	hard	Jul.–Sep.	20 ft (6 m)
C. o. 'Bill Mackenzie'	small, yellow	any aspect	hard	Jul.–Sep.	20 ft (6 m)
C. o. 'Burford Variety'	small, yellow	any aspect	hard	Aug.–Oct.	15 ft (4.5 m)
C. o. 'Corry'	small, yellow (rather glaucous leaves)	any aspect	hard	Jul.–Aug.; Sep.	20 ft (6 ft)
C. o. 'L & S 13342'	small, yellow	any position	hard	Aug.–Oct.	20 ft (6 m)
C. paniculata	small, white	sheltered	none	Apr.	20 ft (6 m)
C. pitcheri	solitary, violet, urn-shaped	any aspect	hard	Jul.–Sep.	10 ft (3 m)
C. pubescens	small, white, star-shaped	any aspect	hard	Jul.	15 ft (4.5 m)
C. thibetianus	small, lime-green	any aspect	hard	Jul.–Sep.	15 ft (4.5 m)
C. × *triternata* 'Rubro-Marginata'	small, deep pink, scented	any aspect	hard	Aug.–Sep.	20 ft (6 m)
C. veitchiana	small, cream	any aspect	hard	Jul.–Sep.	20 ft (6 m)
C. virginiana	small, white	any aspect	hard	Jun.–Jul.	20 ft (6 m)
C. vitalba	small, white	any aspect	hard	Jul.–Oct.	30 ft (9 m)

Africa is represented by *Clematis brachiata* — a vigorous, almost evergreen climber with white-flushed green flowers and a slight scent.

The most scented species of all, however, is *Clematis flammula*, which comes from Europe. Its growth is very vigorous, and the small white star-like flowers give off the most wonderful vanilla scent in midsummer.

Also from Europe is the semi-herbaceous *Clematis integrifolia*. This is best grown over a low wall, where its bright-blue bell-shaped flowers, recurved at the tips, can be seen to best effect.

Above: *Old man's beard (*Clematis vitalba*) can still be found growing in the wild.*

Below: *Here* Clematis vitalba *is seen growing through a conifer, its white flowers shown to advantage.*

The only species native to Britain, *Clematis vitalba*, is probably better known for its display of seed heads than for its flowers, which are usually disappointingly small and off-white in colour. It is the seed heads that have earned it the common name of old man's beard. They make a wonderful autumn display along country roadsides, where after a heavy dew the fluffy tassels glisten in the early morning sun.

America is the home of the popular *Clematis texensis*, much prized for its brilliant scarlet, tubular flowers. It is unfortunately a rather weak grower, and the hybrids are probably a better choice for the garden.

Clematis *'Duchess of Sutherland'* is one of the best of the summer hybrids.

Other climbers

Climbing plants are often thought of merely as the poor relations of garden plants, so that they are generally relegated to the back of plant catalogues. Here they languish, often unnoticed and unappreciated, until a shed or wall needs covering — at which point the ubiquitous Russian

vine or Virginia creeper is brought into action.

Climbers simply do not deserve such treatment. There's a whole multitude of species and varieties just waiting to be discovered — plants that will add colour to an otherwise dowdy tree or shrub; plants to brighten up hedges; and plants that can be allowed to scramble along the ground to provide ground cover.

Rosa 'Alchymist' is an unusual climbing rose with light-yellow flowers that deepen to orange in the centre.

Many climbers have fragrant flowers, whose perfume wafts around the garden on warm spring or summer evenings. Other climbers bear edible fruits in profusion. And many of them will occupy very little space, and will take up very little of your valuable time.

The table on pages 36–37 lists just some of the many species and varieties. Most are readily available from nurseries and garden centres, whereas others will need to be sought out from specialist growers. But all of them are worth growing, and all of them will give you years of pleasure for very little effort.

Climbing herbaceous plants

The plants listed in the table below are all herbaceous. This means that each year they will die down to the base and shoot again the following spring from ground level.

The Chilean flame flower (Tropaeolum speciosum) *bears hosts of bright-scarlet flowers, but can be difficult to establish.*

Lathyrus rotundifolius *is an extremely attractive climbing pea.*

A selection of herbaceous climbers

Species or cultivar	Description	Position	Flowering time	Growth height
Aconitum volubile	lilac-blue, hooded flowers	sunny, good soil	late summer	9 ft (3 m)
Codonopsis convolvulacea	periwinkle-blue, bell-shaped flowers	best in partial shade, fertile soil, cool	late summer	6 ft (2 m)
Dicentra scandens	yellow, pendant blooms	moist, fertile soil	summer	3 ft (1 m)
Lathyrus latifolius	pink flowers (perennial pea of cottage gardens)	sunny	all summer	6 ft (2 m)
L. rotundifolius	pink clusters of flowers	most aspects	summer	6 ft (2 m)
Tropaeolum speciosum (Chilean flame flower)	profuse bright-scarlet flowers; hard to establish	can become invasive in cool moist situations	all summer	12 ft (3.5 m)

A selection of climbers

Species or cultivar	Description	Position	Height	Spread
Abutilon megapotamicum	red-and-yellow flowers with purple anthers	best on warm wall	3 ft (1 m)	3 ft (1 m)
A. m. 'Variegatum'	leaves mottled with yellow; red-and-yellow flowers shaped rather like Turk's cap	sunny, warm wall, well drained	6 ft (2 m)	3 ft (1 m)
Actinidia chinensis 'Haywood' (Chinese gooseberry)	large, hairy leaves with red stems; (female variety: plant with male to develop fruit)	sunny, well drained	9 ft (3 m)	6 ft (2 m)
A. c. 'Tomuri' (Chinese gooseberry)	large, hairy leaves with red stems; (male variety for planting with female)	sunny, well drained	9 ft (3 m)	6 ft (2 m)
A. kolomikta	leaves green splashed with strawberry pink and cream; very exotic-looking	sunny aspect to obtain best colouring	9 ft (3 m)	6 ft (2 m)
Akebia quinata	fragrant, chocolate-purple flowers in spring; usually semi-evergreen	sun or light shade	9 ft (3 m)	15 ft (4.5 m)
Ampelopsis brevipedunculata 'Elegans'	leaves mottled white and pink; not very vigorous; best used as scrambler for limited ground cover	sheltered (somewhat tender)	—	—
Aristolochia macrophylla (Dutchman's pipe)	purple-brown flowers in June; tropical-looking yet quite hardy	sunny, warm wall	12 ft (4 m)	6 ft (2 m)
Billardiera longiflora	greenish-yellow flowers; bright-blue berries later	sunny wall, well drained	6 ft (2 m)	3 ft (1 m)
Calystegia hederacea 'Flore Pleno' (a double bindweed)	shell-pink double flowers during summer; can be invasive, but worth the risk for its profusion of flowers	sunny, well drained	6 ft (2 m)	6 ft (2 m)
Campsis radicans 'Flava' (trumpet vine)	rich-yellow waxy flowers during August	sunny wall to flower best	15 ft (4.5 m)	6 ft (2 m)
C. × *tagliabuana* 'Mme Galen'	salmon-red flowers in late summer	sunny wall	15 ft (4.5 m)	6 ft (2 m)
Celastrus scandens	orange fruits with scarlet seeds; grow up mature tree; plant in pairs to get berries	sun or shade	23 ft (7 m)	12 ft (3.5 m)
Cissus striata	glossy dark-green leaves (evergreen); red/purple fruits	warm, sunny wall	12 ft (3.5 m)	9 ft (3 m)
Eccremocarpus scaber	orange/scarlet tubular flowers June–October	well drained; south- or west-facing	6 ft (2 m)	6 ft (2 m)

Species or cultivar	Description	Position	Height	Spread
Eccremocarpus scaber 'Aurea'	yellow tubular flowers during summer	sunny, well drained	6 ft (2 m)	3 ft (1 m)
Fallopia baldschuanica (Russian vine)	frothy white flower panicles in late summer; very easy to grow though very vigorous	any aspect	40 ft (12 m)	26 ft (8 m)
Hedera colchica (Persian ivy)	large evergreen leaves; good for covering shady banks	any aspect	18 ft (5.5 m)	9 ft (3 m)
H. c. 'Dentata Variegata'	green/grey leaves margined cream; good for ground cover	partial shade	9 ft (3 m)	9 ft (3 m)
H. c. 'Paddy's Pride'	yellow-edged evergreen leaves; avoid heavy shade	sun or light shade	9 ft (3 m)	9 ft (3 m)
H. helix 'Buttercup' (common ivy)	young foliage suffused with yellow; not very vigorous	sunny	9 ft (3 m)	9 ft (3 m)
H. h. 'Cavendishii' (common ivy)	cream-margined evergreen leaves; good cultivar; can also be used as ground cover	sun or shade	15 ft (4.5 m)	12 ft (3.5 m)
H. h. 'Cristata'	young leaves crinkled and bright green; evergreen; looks superb in winter	sun or shade	12 ft (3.5 m)	6 ft (2 m)
Humulus lupulus 'Aureus' (golden hop)	golden foliage in summer	sunny for best colour	15 ft (4.5 m)	6 ft (2 m)
Hydrangea petiolaris (climbing hydrangea)	large white flowers in June; self-clinging	shady wall; moist soil	18 ft (5.5 m)	18 ft (5.5 m)
Jasminum officinale	masses of fragrant pure-white flowers in July	sunny	9 ft (3 m)	6 ft (2 m)
J. × stephanense	fragrant pale-pink flowers June–July	warm, sunny wall	23 ft (7 m)	12 ft (3.5 m)
Lonicera alseuosmoïdes	small yellow-and-purple flowers; evergreen	sunny, well drained	9 ft (3 m)	5 ft (1.5 m)
L. caprifolia 'Anne Fletcher'	large waxy cream flowers; very fragrant	sunny	5 ft (1.5 m)	6 ft (2 m)
L. etrusca	fragrant cream/yellow flowers; semi-evergreen	sunny	9 ft (3 m)	6 ft (2 m)
L. heckrotii 'Gold Flame'	orange-yellow flowers July–August	most aspects	12 ft (3.5 m)	6 ft (2 m)
L. periclymenum 'Graham Thomas' (common honeysuckle)	masses of cream-coloured flowers in July; very fragrant	sunny	9 ft (3 m)	6 ft (2 m)
Vitis 'Brant'	sweet, aromatic grapes, then glorious autumn colours	sunny, warm wall	25 ft (9 m)	15 ft (4.5 m)
V. coignetiae	large heart-shaped leaves; fiery autumn colours; vigorous but can be trimmed annually	sun or shade	23 ft (7 m)	12 ft (3.5 m)

Soils

The better the soil, the more success you will have with your clematis and climbers. Alas, there are very few gardens with really good soil. But fortunately there is such a wide choice of plants available these days that you will be able to grow something, no matter how poor your soil is.

Garden compost and manure

Your garden soil can also be improved quite dramatically over a period of time by adding organic material in the form of well-rotted manure or garden compost. If your soil is dry and sandy, then either of these materials will eventually make it more water-retentive. Heavy clay soils will also become easier to work, provided you only use manure that contains a high proportion of straw.

The primary object is to retain as much water as possible during the growing season but to allow excess water to drain away freely during the dormant period. If you dig in plenty of organic matter before planting, this should start the

ball rolling. Follow this up with annual mulches of manure, compost or bark when the soil is moist, and you will eventually have the perfect growing medium.

Feeding and fertilisers

It is a myth that clematis need lime in order to grow satisfactorily. Many species in fact grow on very acid soils in their native countries, and all clematis will tolerate a wide range of pH values. On the other hand, what they do require is large amounts of nutrients.

The word 'compost' is potentially confusing because it has two quite different meanings:

- a balanced mixture of different kinds of soil for the cultivation of plants grown in pots or other containers

- a valuable material made by rotting down vegetable or plant refuse.

Throughout this book we have tried to avoid any ambiguity in the use of the term 'compost'.

Flowering climbers such as Wisteria sinensis *will benefit from fertilisers that are high in potash.*

Clematis are greedy feeders and impossible to overfeed. However, if you want them to give of their best and provide an abundant display of flowers, then you should avoid nitrogenous fertilisers in favour of those which are high in potash. The perfect fertilisers are those designed for roses. If you apply these at the same strength and with the same frequency, this will ensure a magnificent show year after year.

Potash has been described as 'sunshine in a bottle' — a very apt description for the plant food that not only makes plants flower freely but also increases the depth of colour in the flowers. It also improves the plants' winter hardiness by stimulating them to make sugars in the sap, which raises the freezing point in much the same way as anti-freeze in a car. So watering with tomato fertiliser every other week will also improve your clematis.

What's good for clematis is also good for other climbers. Indeed, the same treatment can be applied to most climbers. The flowering climbers such as wisterias will certainly benefit. However, some caution is needed when feeding plants grown for their foliage — especially evergreens such as the ivies. Too much fertiliser will make them grow more than you perhaps require, and can also lead to soft growth that is liable to be scorched by the sun or by cold winter winds.

Bomarea caldasii — *a herbaceous twining climber with distinctive tubular flowers (see page 35)*

Planting

All climbers these days are grown and sold in pots. Then, provided the ground is neither too dry nor too cold, you can plant them out at any time of the year.

Buying the right plant

Before you can start planting, you first have to purchase the right plant, and this is where a lot of gardeners make those choices that so often lead to failure. It's all too easy to be carried away by a plant cover-ed in flowers, and to forget that what you really need is a good set of roots with some well-balanced top growth. Plants often flower profusely in pots if they've been neglected. They think they are going to die, so produce copious amounts of flower in order to set seed. Such plants seldom thrive, or at best they take time to settle down.

You also need to make sure the plant is 'nursery-fresh' by looking at the top layer of compost. If it has a caked appearance, or if there are weeds growing or a layer of moss, then don't buy the plant. These are all signs of neglect at some stage, as is a lack of leaves or yellowing on the growing stems.

Clematis, particularly some of the hybrids, will naturally throw out roots from the base of the pot; this is perfectly acceptable provided all the other conditions are met. Honeysuckles, on the other hand, really loathe being pot-bound, and can sulk for years if they have been planted in this condition.

Planting procedure

Although clematis and other climbers can be planted out at any time of the year, the best time to do this is undoubtedly the early spring, when the soil has warmed up but is still relatively moist.

With most climbers you should dig a hole a couple of spits deep and a spade and a half in width. Incorporate a good amount of well-rotted compost or other organic matter into the base of the hole, place the plant in the hole and fill up with soil until the soil ball of the plant is slightly below the surface.

Clematis, however, require a very different sort of treatment. They are best planted somewhat deeper than other climbers, allowing a few buds to remain below the soil level. This procedure will enable the roots to put up new shoots if the top of the plant dies, and it also makes for a much bushier and sturdier plant.

Once you have worked out the optimum planting depth, knock the plant carefully out of its pot, taking great care not to break any of the stems. Then immediately place it in position, still taking care so as not to disturb the soil ball.

First place a small quantity of soil around the plant in order to keep it nicely stable. Then start to fill in the planting hole by breaking down the sides with a fork. This stops the soil around the plant becoming compacted, and is more important with heavier soils. If the sides of the hole are too compacted, they can act almost like the walls of a pot, eventually stopping the plant from developing. As you replace the soil, firm it in gently, preferably with the heel of your foot. This is to bring the plant into good contact with the soil without destroying the structure of the soil (using the whole foot can do just that).

Finally, tidy up around the plant and then water it. Even if the soil is already moist, the action of the water will help to wash the soil around the roots so that the plant settles in straight away.

Three stages of the procedure — planting **(far left)**, *staking* **(left)** *and tying in a clematis plant* **(right)**

Propagation

Of all the many and varied gardening tasks, the propagation of plants must rank amongst the most satisfying. But whether you want to produce one plant or hundreds of them, the same principles apply, the first of which is attention to detail.

Timing and record-keeping

Even if you do adhere to all the principles, your first few attempts (certainly with cuttings) will probably not be a great triumph. However, if you do fail first time round, then this will most likely be due to poor timing.

Plants mature according to the seasons, and seeds and cuttings are greatly influenced by changes in weather conditions. During a dry period, for instance, the seed will ripen very quickly, while a stem that is ideal for cuttings will very quickly harden, greatly reducing the chances of its taking root successfully.

Wet weather presents its own set of problems: the seed may rot on the plant, while cutting material may be so full of water that it rots and dies back.

For this reason it is always a good idea to keep a diary or some form of gardening log. If you note down all your successes and failures, together with the time of the year and the prevailing weather conditions, then a pattern will gradually emerge. The data will be extremely valuable, enabling you to increase the percentage of successes and also to monitor the exact requirements for each individual plant.

Healthy plant material

It is equally important that you should only use material from healthy and well-grown plants. Any plant that is suffering from starvation, poor growing conditions, disease or insect attack should simply be rejected. The seed will probably not have matured, and any cutting material will have already been damaged.

For the same reason it's important to feed and water your potential parent plants even more carefully than the rest. They are, after all, going to provide for the next generation. But when feeding them, you should err on the side of caution as far as nitrogen-based fertilisers are concerned.

After inserting cuttings in a flower pot, place a polythene bag over the pot to retain warmth and moisture.

Concentrate on well-balanced fertilisers with a higher percentage of potash, and you will produce sturdier, healthier plants. Nitrogen promotes growth, but if used in excess it also tends to make the material very soft and sappy, and therefore liable to disease. Potash, on the other hand, increases the sugars in the sap, and this not only promotes hardiness but also aids propagation.

Cleanliness

Whatever tools you use, you must always clean them thoroughly before carrying out each new task. Cleanliness is the overriding principle here. All too often, perfectly healthy seeds and good cuttings have gone to waste simply because of inadequate hygiene. Sometimes the compost used has been infected with weeds or diseases, or the cutting tools have become infected from other plants.

It doesn't take long to wave a knife blade through a gentle flame, or to wash your pots and seed trays in a mild disinfectant. Yet these simple measures alone are enough to produce a dramatic increase in the number of plants that can be successfully propagated.

Always ask permission

This is one principle that gardeners feel very strongly

There must be millions of 'Nelly Moser' specimens, yet all of them have been propagated from a single original plant.

about. Never take seeds or cutting material from any plant without the owner's permission. Other people's gardens, especially those of the rich and famous, may contain some wonderful plants. But don't be tempted, as so many people are, to take cuttings from a plant in the hope that no one will mind.

The resulting condition is euphemistically known as finger blight — a well-known disease that affects plants growing in gardens that are open to the public. Remember that the gardener may well choose these plants for the very same purpose, only to discover that some unthinking person has removed all the prime cutting material.

The seed heads of Clematis tangutica *can be seen here amid the berries of a cotoneaster.*

Gardeners, almost without exception, are very generous creatures, and if you ask them they will probably give you far more material than you ever expected.

Carrying the plant material
There remains the problem of how to get the seed or cutting material back home in good condition. For seed an envelope or paper bag is ideal —

not polythene, as this can create problems of overheating or condensation.

For cutting material, there is a handy transportation method that can be used over long periods without the material coming to any harm. Take a polythene bag, dip it in water, shake off the excess and place the propagation material inside. Then blow air into the bag, seal it and place it in a shady place.

Seed propagation

Propagating plants from seed is a cheap if not always reliable means of increasing plants. While plants grown from the seed collected from species will be more or less true to type, the seeds from hybrids will inevitably produce totally new hybrids.

The latter can be a useful way of producing new varieties, especially if you've carefully planned the hybridisation and chosen the parents with a view to the final goal. However, it can also lead to disappointments, even among the species. *Clematis tangutica*, for instance, will show marked differences in flower shape and colour when grown from seed. *C. viticella*, although very easy to germinate, often produces plants with small, muddy-coloured flowers of little decorative value.

So much for the negative side of growing from seed. In the main, however, it is great fun, and while the results — espe-

When raised from seed, a Clematis tangutica *may look noticeably different from the parent plant.*

cially with clematis — may not be what you intend, you will often be surprised. You may even fall on an all-time winner such as a red tangutica or a beautifully scented large-flowered hybrid.

The time taken for clematis seed to ripen depends on the species and on the time of flowering. As the seeds ripen, they each develop a feathery tail that is normally used for wind dispersal. Then is the time to harvest the seed. As soon as you've collected enough seed, carefully remove the tassels, place your seed in a polythene bag together with some moist sand, and keep it in the refrigerator at just below 40°F (4.5°C) until the following spring.

Once the weather starts to warm up, remove the seed-and-sand mixture from the fridge and prepare a seed tray or pot with some good-quality seed compost. Gently firm it down, and lightly sprinkle the seed and sand over the surface. Give the tray a good watering, cover it with a sheet of glass or polythene, and place it in a shady place well away from marauding mice (who love clematis seeds).

With some clematis varieties, germination can take 12 months or even longer. Once germination has taken place,

give the new seedlings more light before potting them on into small pots. At this point it's a good idea to start feeding the seedlings. Give each of them a weak liquid feed, and insert a small cane up which the young plant can then start to grow.

Keep your clematis seedlings watered at all times, because they are now at their most vulnerable. As they start to grow — and certainly within a couple of months — they will need transplanting into a slightly larger pot. At this stage it pays to pot them into a fairly

45

rich compost, burying a few buds in the same way as if you were planting them out. This will allow the plants to produce even more roots. Also, provided you pinch out the top growth, they will produce nice bushy plants ready for planting out the following spring.

You'll have to wait three or four years before your clematis will flower, so it's not a project for the faint-hearted. But always bear in mind that many of the best modern introductions have come from chance seedlings. You never know — yours might be the next one!

Clematis from cuttings

If you need to add several plants your stock, then propagation from cuttings is probably the most reliable method, if not the easiest.

The main advantage of taking cuttings is that all the plants produced will be the same as the original source of the material. They are known as clones, and share all the characteristics of the parent plant. It can be argued that they are in fact the same plant. The millions of plants of the variety 'Nelly Moser', for instance, can all be tracked back to one single plant.

There are three important points to follow when growing plants from cuttings:

1 Always choose the healthiest and best-grown plant from which to take your cuttings.

Clematis macropetala *'Markhams Pink'* is a good candidate for raising from cuttings.

You will be wasting your time and effort if you try to use material that is yellow from starvation, or thin and weak from being left in the shade.

2 Use a very sharp blade to work with. One of the many craft knives available is ideal, as are single-sided razor blades. Keep the blade scrupulously clean and sharp, and cut the material as cleanly as you can. A ragged cut when detaching material can allow diseases to enter, which can damage the parent plant.

3 Keep the cutting material firm until it is safely in the propagator. Once the material has been detached from the parent, it will not be able to take up water again until it has formed its own roots.

Once you've detached your stem, observing these first three points, the next stage is to trim the stem into individual cuttings. Clematis are usually rooted using *internodal* cuttings — i.e. those taken from the sections of stem between the leaves. This is simply so that you can obtain as many cuttings as possible from a given length of stem. Clematis will in fact root just as readily from *nodal* cuttings — i.e. those from the area immediately around the base of each leaf. The choice is yours.

Take your very sharp blade and simply cut the stem into lengths. Cut between the leaves, and again immediately above them, taking care not to damage the buds in the leaf axil. Given that the cutting must not be allowed to wilt, you can reduce the risk of this by carefully cutting off one of the leaves.

Now insert your cutting into some moist cuttings compost. For small quantities a small pot is the best container to use, with the cuttings spaced evenly around the edge (for some reason they don't root so well in the centre of the pot). In the case of internodal cuttings, the leaf base should rest at or just below the surface. With nodal cuttings the leaf base should be well below the surface. Continue with this procedure until you've inserted all your cuttings. Then water them well and cover with polythene.

Give your cuttings plenty of light — but never direct sunlight — and occasionally spray them over with a light mist of water. If all goes well, they should have rooted within a month or so.

What varieties to use and when

The easiest clematis varieties to root, and the best ones to start off with, are the alpinas, macropetalas and montanas. If you take cuttings from these in the spring, they will develop into sturdy plants before the winter, and can be over-wintered in their pots before being planted out the following spring.

The large-flowered hybrids, and cultivars from other species, are more difficult to manage but still worth trying. These will take longer to root, so great patience is needed. There's nothing worse for a cutting than being constantly removed from its compost for inspection; then its chances of survival will be virtually nil. If the cuttings have not rooted well by mid-August, then it's better to leave them *in situ* until the following spring, when they will have a better chance of becoming estab-lished. If you do this, then you should keep a regular check on the pots, clearing the soil surface of dead leaves during the autumn months to prevent disease striking.

Propagation by layering

The most foolproof method of propagating clematis, and a wide range of climbers besides, is the technique known as layering.

The basic method is very simple: you select a stem from the parent plant that can easily reach the ground and trail along it; then you place a portion of the stem under the soil and wait for it to root. However, there are a few extra precautions worth considering, as these will raise your chances of success to almost 100 percent.

Cuttings of Clematis montana

The basic principle is fine so long as your garden soil is in perfect condition. If not, then you should fill a medium-sized pot with a good-quality compost — John Innes, for example — and sink this at or near the base of the parent plant. Select your stem, lay it across the top of the pot, and cover one or more of the leaf joints or nodes with a little more of the compost. Secure the buried section of the stem with a piece of bent wire inserted into the compost, and water thoroughly.

Make sure the pot is well watered at all times, and within a few months a new shoot will emerge from the covered buds. Once the new plant is growing strongly, it can be detached from the parent and treated as a separate entity.

If the stem you've selected is long enough, you can continue the layering process along the stem, choosing alternate nodes. But as the plants take root, always remember not to detach any of them on the side towards the parent plant until all those on the other side are properly rooted.

Supports

All climbers by their very nature need supports, and these supports must be strong enough to do the job for a considerable time.

Where plants are grown against a wall, there is now a vast array of different types of trellis available in a variety of materials and designs. These

Above: *This lovely specimen of* Rosa longicuspis *has been trained over three crab-apple stumps ...*

... and within a few years **(below)** *it has grown to form a wonderful living arbour.*

are all very suitable for the purpose. However, unless you are growing an evergreen, you should give some consideration as to what the structure will look like during the winter, when it and not the plant becomes the decorative fixture.

Perhaps the best system for supporting wall-trained plants is to use strong, medium-gauge wire pulled taut between two vine eyes. Such a structure becomes virtually invisible as the plant develops, and provides all the strength and flexibility that both the gardener and the plant require.

Clematis can also look very effective when grown up free-standing pillars. A number of different types of these are available. Made out of hardwood, they will last for many years. But always bear in mind that when a clematis is in full leaf, the support needs to be firmly anchored to the ground to stop the whole structure keeling over in a sudden squall. Don't be tempted to use concrete for this job, as it rots timber far more quickly than anything else. One of the metal spikes used for fence posts is ideal, and can be dug out and moved if necessary.

Wooden supports of all sorts, from arches to fences, need to be maintained from time to time. This is best done during the winter, when the climber is dormant and can be disentangled from its support with a modicum of safety; any shoots that break can be pruned back to a good bud and will soon recover. You should also check what preservative has been used on the wood, and make sure it won't harm the plant.

Creosote, for instance, is lethal to all plant life over a long period. It's far better to use one of the acrylic preservatives, which not only protect the timber but also renew the colour of your structure.

Growing clematis and climbers against walls

Walls are often thought of as the obvious place to grow clematis and climbers. Unfortunately, they are not always the best option. The soil at the base of a wall is frequently dry and impoverished. The wall itself can absorb large quantities of water, which then evaporates so that more is taken up, leaving even less water available to the plants.

Despite these drawbacks, however, there are plants that will grow well in these conditions. If you think carefully and make the right choice of plants, then even the most unglamorous of walls can be made to look more attractive, and the structure of the house will blend harmoniously with the garden.

Clematis on their own, with the possible exception of the montanas, are poorly suited to growing up walls. They tend to loose their bottom leaves as they grow, and very often you are left with a bare and leggy plant, starved of moisture, with just a few scraggy blooms atop

Clematis *'Perle d'Azur'* growing up a wall

A selection of vigorous climbers for walls

Species or cultivar	Flowers/foliage	Position	Flowering time	Growth height	Spread
Clematis chrysocoma	small white blooms	sheltered	May	20 ft (6 m)	—
C. c. 'Hybrid'	small, sugar-pink flowers in profusion	any aspect	Apr.–May	30 ft (9 m)	—
C. c. sericea	small white flowers	any aspect	May	20 ft (6 m)	—
C. montana	small white flowers in profusion	any aspect	Apr.–May	30 ft (10 m)	—
C. m. 'Elizabeth'	small, scented, soft-pink flowers	any aspect	May–Jun.	30 ft (9 m)	—
C. m. 'Freda'	small, cherry-pink blooms with dark edges	any aspect	May–Jun	30 ft (9 m)	—
C. m. 'Grandiflora'	small white flowers	any aspect	May–Jun.	30 ft (9 m)	—
Hedera colchica (Persian ivy)	large, glossy-green evergreen leaves	shady	—	15 ft (4.5 m)	9 ft (3 m)
H. colchica 'Paddy's Pride'	yellow-edged evergreen leaves	sun or light shade	—	9 ft (3 m)	9 ft (3 m)
Hydrangea petiolaris (climbing hydrangea)	large white blooms (self-clinging)	shady wall	Jun.	15 ft (4.5 m)	15 ft (4.5 m)
Parthenocissus henryana	silver-veined leaves; brilliant, fiery autumn colour	any aspect	—	15 ft (4.5m)	6 ft (2 m)
P. quinquefolia (Virginia creeper)	green leaves; superb autumn colour	any aspect	—	20 ft (6 m)	15 ft (4.5 m)
P. tricuspidata 'Veitchii' (Boston ivy)	smaller leaves, but excellent autumn colour	sun or shade (self-clinging)	—	15 ft (4.5 m)	15 ft (4.5 m)

a jumble of stems. In such situations, clematis are always best used in conjunction with other shrubs, the classic example being climbing roses.

A clematis–rose combination provides a display of scented flowers throughout the summer. The clematis spreads throughout its host, its bare lower stems hidden among the roses. A good climbing rose to choose might be *Rosa* 'New Dawn', which has wonderful soft-pink blooms and is less vulnerable to the usual ills of blackspot and mildew. It works well with *Clematis* 'Perle d'Azur', the best late-flowering blue. This particular combination should remain in flower from June until September.

Unsightly walls present a different problem. In such situations the whole wall needs to be covered and hidden completely from view. The vigorous climbers are ideal for this purpose. Boston ivy, Virginia creeper and Russian vine will all make short work of hiding even a quite large area of wall, while the montana group of clematis will provide a flowering screen in the early months of the year.

Evergreen climbers are more difficult. They generally require a protected site away from the effects of cold winds, and this is especially true of the evergreen clematis and the more exotic climbers. However, any of the varieties of our native common ivy (*Hedera helix*) will grow happily against even the coldest wall, and can be readily clipped to keep them under control.

Most climbers require some sort of structure on which to climb up the wall. There is now a wide selection to choose from, ranging from wooden

Above: Lonicera tellmanniana *(centre) is ideal for growing on a shady wall.*

grid trellises to thin plastic netting. Perhaps the best solution, however, is strong medium-gauge wire stretched taut between vine eyes. Equally effective is a pattern of wall nails ranged horizontally to the required width of the plant, and spaced vertically at intervals of about a yard (metre). This method provides adequate support for the plant without becoming an eyesore in the winter months, as is often the case with many of the other systems.

Clematis 'Daniel Deronda' with single flowers (see pages 19–20)

51

Growing clematis and climbers up trees

Growing clematis, indeed any climber, up a tree is often easier said than done. You have to think carefully about the type of tree, and you need to know when your chosen climber will flower and how vigorously it will grow. There is little point in growing a montana through an apple tree, as they will both flower at the same time — and a large-flowered hybrid would simply not be able to cope with the demands of the host tree.

The so-called forest trees such as oak and ash are totally unsuitable for even the most vigorous of climbers, with the possible exception of the more robust roses. The various

Clematis chrysocoma copes well with growing up a conifer.

decorative cherries can also prove a problem as they are surface rooters. This means they take up a lot of the food and water that might otherwise be available to the clematis.

Clematis 'Ville de Lyon' growing through a conifer

Conifers and the smaller garden trees are a different matter altogether. Many of the clematis varieties can add a new perspective to an otherwise dreary specimen, or provide flowers after the host plant finished its display.

When planting a climber to ramble up and through a garden tree, plant it well away from the main stem — preferably just inside the canopy — and lead it up to the branches by means of some stout twine. This will allow the climber to become established outside the dry, impoverished soils around the trunk. Even so, it pays to incorporate plenty of organic matter into the planting hole, and to keep the clematis well watered and fed for the first few seasons.

The same applies to a coniferous host. Plant your climbers away from the main body of the plant and lead them up towards it at an angle. Then they will normally do better

and will also be easier to manage.

The choice of variety is also important for maximum effect. The bigger conifers such as the cultivars of *Chamaecyparis lawsoniana* (Lawson cypress) will cope quite happily with the less vigorous montanas — *Clematis montana* 'Pictons Variety', for instance. For the smaller conifers it is better to choose a late-flowering clematis such as *C.* 'Comtesse de Bouchaud'.

The later-flowering clematis can also be trimmed back in the autumn. The conifer will then look tidier during the winter, while the clematis will be less vulnerable to damage from winter storms.

As clematis use their leaf stems to attach themselves to the host plant, they can often be left to their own devices. But you can often improve the display by using paper-covered wire twists to tie in certain selected stems; this will ensure

that they flower exactly where you want them. It also stops the clematis being dislodged in windy conditions.

Growing clematis and climbers through shrubs

Clematis make ideal subjects for growing through a variety of other shrubs of different sizes. Some of them will extend the period of interest by flowering before or after their host. Others will create an attractive foil for a flowering shrub or one grown for its foliage.

Clematis were very often grown like this in Victorian times. But nowadays, for some strange reason, it is no longer the first idea that springs to mind when we think of growing clematis, or indeed any climbing plant.

Some shrubs are more difficult to match than others. Lilacs and rhododendrons, for instance, are almost impossible

A selection of climbers for growing through shrubs

Species or cultivar	Flowers	Position	Flowering time	Growth height	Spread
Calystegia hederacea 'Flore Pleno'	double, shell-pink	sunny, well drained	summer	6 ft (2 m)	can be invasive
Eccremocarpus scaber	orange/scarlet	sunny, well drained	Jun.–Oct.	6 ft (2 m)	6 ft (2 m)
Lonicera tellmanniana	bright orange, tubular	shady	Jul.	12 ft (3.5 m)	9 ft (3 m)
L. × *americana*	long, fragrant with purple outers	sunny	—	15 ft (4.5 m)	12 ft (3.4 m)
Solanum jasminoides 'Album'	white with yellow beak	warm, sunny	summer	9 ft (3 m)	6 ft (2 m)

A selection of clematis for growing through shrubs

Cultivar	Flowers	Position	Pruning needed	Flowering time	Growth height
C. 'Bees Jubilee'	large, deep pink with rose bar	shady	light	May–Jun.; Aug.	10 ft (3 m)
C. 'Comtesse de Bouchaud'	large, mauve-pink	any aspect	hard	Jul.–Aug.	10 ft (3 m)
C. 'Dawn'	large, pearly-pink	shady	light	May–Jun.; Aug.	10 ft (3 m)
C. 'Dr Ruppel'	large, pink with deeper bar	shady	light	May–Jul.	10 ft (3 m)
C. 'Fireworks'	violet-mauve with carmine bar	any aspect	light	Jun.–Aug.	15 ft (4.5 m)
C. 'General Sikorsky'	large, mid-blue	any aspect	light	Jun.–July.	10 ft (3 m)
C. 'Gillian Blades'	large, white with faint mauve edge	any aspect	light	May–Jun.; Sep.	12 ft (3.5 m)
C. 'H. F. Young'	large, wedgwood blue	any aspect	light	May–Jun.	10 ft (3 m)
C. 'Hagley Hybrid'	medium, rosy/mauve	any aspect	hard	Jun.–Aug.	8 ft (3.5 m)
C. 'Haku Ookan'	large, violet, with cream anthers	any aspect	light	May–Jun.; Sep.	12 ft (3.5 m)
C. 'Perle d'Azur'	medium, azure-blue	any aspect	hard	Jul.–Sep.	15 ft (4.5 m)

to link successfully with clematis because of their fibrous surface roots. But with most combinations you are unlikely to encounter any problems.

One of the most effective ideas is to combine clematis with one of the old-fashioned roses. Most of these wonderful plants have only a short flowering period, so grouping them with clematis makes for a wonderful combination, adding scent, colour and structure to even the smallest garden.

Perhaps the best candidates for this purpose are the later-flowering clematis hybrids; these can be pruned back hard, which means the rose is less of a nightmare to prune than might otherwise be the case.

Lower-growing shrubs such as weigelas, cotinus (if pruned annually) or the smaller mock oranges (*Philadelphus* spp.) are suitable with early large-flowered and double hybrids. *Clematis* 'Miss Bateman', a pure-white variety, looks superb growing through the rich-purple foliage of *Cotinus coggygria* 'Royal Purple'. The texensis varieties lend themselves well to scrambling through the branches of low-

Below and **below left:** *The white flowers of* Clematis *'Miss Bateman' stand out wonderfully against the rich-purple foliage of* Cotinus coggygria *'Royal Purple'.*

Above: Clematis *'Rouge Cardinal' growing through* Penstemon *'Hidcote Pink'*

growing shrubs, where you can look down into their tulip-shaped flowers.

The taller shrubs don't necessarily demand vigorous clematis. Some of the more compact clematis varieties will provide colour around the lower branches of shrubs that might otherwise be bereft of interest. Examples of these include the

hybrid *Clematis* 'Royalty', with its gorgeous plum-purple semi-double blooms, and *C.* 'H. F. Young', which has light-blue single flowers.

Many climbers are too vigorous for growing through any but the largest and most robust shrubs. But there are a few exceptions to this: the double pink bindweed *Calystegia hederacea* 'Flore Pleno', and also some of the honeysuckles, can be just as effective when allowed to mingle through the branches of another plant.

Growing clematis as ground cover

The term ground cover has come to be applied to those plants which provide a tight mat of foliage at ground level, thus inhibiting weed growth. Although clematis can provide many benefits, it has to be said that this is not one of them.

The foliage of most clematis is simply not dense enough to keep unwanted weeds at bay. The one notable exception is *Clematis × jouiniana* 'Praecox', whose thick layers of leaves completely cover the surface during the summer months. Otherwise, clematis as ground cover has more decorative than practical value.

In the wild, clematis will naturally scramble along the ground until it meets some form of support up which to climb. This tendency can be used to great effect in the garden, where clematis can spread over quite large areas and produce a riot of colour for several months.

Clematis can also be used in conjunction with heathers and other ground-cover plants; winter-flowering varieties are especially suitable. When growing clematis with heathers, it's best to plant them so that they grow initially through a clay land drain. This gives the clematis some height, and also protects the young plants from the attentions of mice. These rodents love using heathers for their winter quarters, and can remove the clematis shoots at ground level each winter.

The best clematis for growing with heathers are the later-flowering varieties, particularly the viticella hybrids that flower on the current season's growth. This means you can prune back the clematis in the autumn, allowing the heathers to flower unencumbered by the tangle of old clematis shoots. The heathers can also

Clematis viticella *and its cultivars make excellent ground-cover plants.*

Suggested clematis for ground cover

Cultivar	Flowers	Position	Pruning needed	Flowering time
Clematis × jouiniana 'Praecox'	small, lavender	any aspect	hard	Jul.–Sep.
C. viticella 'Abundance'	small, red	any aspect	hard	Jul.–Sep.
C. v. 'Alba Luxurians'	small, creamy-white	any aspect	hard	Jul.–Sep.
C. v. 'Etoile Violette'	medium, violet	any aspect	hard	Jul.–Sep.
C. v. 'Kermesina'	small, red	any aspect	hard	Jul.–Aug.
C. v. 'Mme Julia Correvon'	small, wine-red	any aspect	hard	Jul.–Aug.
C. v. 'Margot Koster'	small, rosy-red, profuse	any aspect	hard	Aug.–Sep.

have their annual haircut in the spring before the clematis has got into its stride. The result will be a truly well-balanced relationship, providing colour from foliage and flowers for all twelve months of the year.

The later-flowering clematis hybrids can also be used on their own. Varieties such as *Clematis viticella* 'Abundance' and *C. v.* 'Etoile Violette' will scramble happily along the ground. However, the stems should be pegged down every so often with pieces of bent wire so as to prevent them being blown into a useless tangle by summer winds. Early spring bulbs can be under-planted to extend the flowering period.

The early-summer large-flowered varieties can also be used in this way, but these require light pruning, which is much more fiddly. Also, the flowers tend to be eaten by slugs and earwigs. As a result they are better suited to growing up other plants or various structures.

Clematis henryi planted as ground cover

Pruning clematis

Pruning is a technique which over the years has gained a certain mystique, and which for some reason has been made increasingly complicated. There is no logical basis for this, as it is essentially a very simple operation.

The first important principle to understand is that the plants themselves have no wish to be pruned. They will live out their lives quite happily without ever being snipped or cut. Pruning is purely for the gardener's benefit and not for the plants.

If clematis are left unpruned, they will naturally continue growing year after year until they reach their full height. At the same time they will produce side shoots at a prodigious rate, and these will become progressively thinner and weaker as the years progress. The whole plant will also age from the bottom upwards. This in turn will mean that all the flowers will be produced at the top, and will become much smaller as the shoots become weaker.

The purpose of pruning, therefore, is to create a well-balanced plant which flowers as and where you want it. You may also be to able to control flowering time to some extent.

Pruning is an operation that if possible should be undertaken when you are in a particularly good mood, and when all seems well with the world. This is because clematis are fiddly things to deal with, and when enmeshed in other plants they can try the patience

To keep it in bounds, Clematis montana *should be pruned hard every summer.*

of a saint. Secateurs are also sharp and dangerous, and when your concentration lapses it is all too easy to remove the wrong sections of plants — and bodies!

With clematis, as with plants of any description, there are two main factors that determine when and how they should be pruned: the time of flowering, and whether flowers are produced on old or new growth. For this reason clematis are generally divided into three categories for the purposes of pruning:

Summer pruning

Clematis that require summer pruning are those that bloom early in the year on the previous year's growth, which will have ripened during the summer. This category includes the montana, alpina, macropetala and evergreen varieties, all of which finish flowering by June.

Because these types of clematis are grown for covering large areas, they are often left unpruned. They continue to flower happily for many years until they eventually outgrow their allotted space, at which point they are hacked back with a venom that would do justice to Attila the Hun. Several more years pass before the poor plant can produce enough wood for any sort of display, and then the whole process is carried out again.

Yet such a scenario could so easily be avoided by a little judicious pruning — removing all dead wood and any weak growth, and cutting back some of the side shoots immediately after flowering.

With montanas you can be quite severe. One of the most pleasing spring sights one can encounter is a *Clematis montana* 'Elizabeth' forming a pink tracery around a cottage door and window. Such a display can be maintained by keeping a basic framework of old wood and pruning the current season's shoots back quite hard in June. This also has the effect of increasing the flower size considerably, creating an even more spectacular and eye-catching display.

If you happen to have a neglected plant in this category, then instead of cutting it hard back all in one go, it's much better to tackle the problem over a couple of seasons. Begin in year one by removing as many as possible of the dead and tangled shoots, and then cut back the plant by about one-third. During the following growing season the clematis will form new shoots from the old growth, some of it quite low down on the plant. In year two, after you have once again enjoyed the flowers, remove any really old and gnarled wood, some of it to ground level if necessary, to make way for the newly rejuvenated portions.

The evergreen varieties, and *Clematis armandii* in particular, tend to benefit from an annual prune. They always look unkempt after flowering, and also become very bare at the base. The removal of the old flowering stems will do wonders. *C. armandii*, despite its reputation for being delicate, is surprisingly vigorous: an annual prune will encourage far more growth than is removed, all of which will flower the following season.

There is a saying that sums up this section: if they flower before June, there is no need to prune — but if you remove all the old and dead growth, the results will more than pay for the time invested.

Light annual pruning

The clematis that require this type of pruning are those which begin flowering in May or June and tend to finish by August. They produce the bulk of their blooms on wood that has been produced the previous year, but if they flower a second time it happens on the current year's shoots.

This is the group that creates the most confusion for gardeners, mainly because experts propose so many different solutions to the problem. However, at the risk of labouring the point, remember that you are pruning for *your* benefit and not for the plant. If you bear this maxim in mind, then the procedure will be much easier to follow.

The timing is quite important. If you wish to obtain the

maximum benefit, you should prune some time in the early spring — say, late February or early March — just as the buds are beginning to swell. At this stage you will be able to distinguish between two distinct types of bud: those which are nicely plump and will carry the first flowers, and the smaller, less pronounced types, which will only provide shoots.

The first task is to disentangle the clematis from its host plant as much as you can, and to remove any dead, diseased or weak growth. Having done this, you can then remove a portion of the remaining shoots down to a pair of flowering buds at the point where you want the clematis to flower. Carry on doing this until you have dealt with all the main stems. There may some stems that don't possess any

Two cultivars that will benefit from a light annual prune — Clematis *'Lincoln Star'* **(right)** *and C. 'Kathleen Wheeler'* **(below)**

flowering buds at all, in which case they will come to no harm if you prune them back quite hard. This will encourage the plant to produce more basal shoots, which may well flower later in the season.

Victorian gardeners used to use this method to increase the flowering span of varieties such as *Clematis* 'Nelly Moser', which normally flowers twice in the season — once in May or June and again around August time. If they pruned part of the plant lightly and the other part of the plant severely, they could obtain flowers in July as well.

At some stage you may inherit a neglected plant of one of these varieties, or perhaps one year you are unable to prune. A clematis that hasn't been pruned regularly is an all too familiar sight — all denuded at the base, and with a mare's nest of small, weak shoots at the top. If such is the case, then the best course of action is to prune the plant hard in early spring, preferably avoiding any really old and mature wood, and start again almost from scratch. As a result of this seemingly brutish act, the clematis will throw up an abundance of

shoots from the base. They may or may not flower the first year, but the following year they are certain to provide a glorious show. For by then the plant will have been completely rejuvenated.

Hard pruning
Clematis that require hard pruning are among the most attractive of all garden plants. Because they flower on the shoots of the current year's

Clematis *'Mme Edouard André'* is a cultivar that needs hard pruning.

Clematis tangutica can be left unpruned for several years, but eventually it deteriorates as the old, unproductive wood starts to predominate. Here it is seen growing next to a cotoneaster, which sets off its yellow flowers nicely.

growth, they provide an abundance of flowers during the latter part of summer. Consequently, as they take all summer to produce their flower buds, they require a hard prune every year if only to keep them in some sort of control.

This group comprises the varieties of *Clematis viticella,* many of the species such as *C. tangutica,* and also the herbaceous types. The viticellas are very well suited to growing through a variety of other trees and shrubs, while the species are useful for covering large areas such as unsightly sheds or fences. This means that different pruning strategies are required to suit different purposes.

When plants are used for growing up poles and conifers, you generally want them to start flowering as low down as possible. On the other hand, not many gardeners want to look out of a window during the cold winter months to see a mass of dormant twigs clinging haphazardly to a fine specimen of golden conifer.

These plants should ideally be pruned in the early spring — or to be more precise, some time around late February or early March, just as the sap is rising and the buds are beginning to swell. If they have been regularly pruned, then at this time of the year they will produce large buds about six inches (15 cm) above the base. You should prune down to these basal buds, as they contain all the necessary vigour to provide the profusion of flowers that makes these clematis so popular. If you prune too early, however, this can lead to premature soft growth, which can be damaged by frost or cold winds. So it's important to do this job at exactly the right time.

This still leaves the problem of the golden conifer. If the tree is to provide any pleasure in the winter, then the stems of the preceding year's growth need be removed during the autumn instead of the spring. The best solution to this dilemma is to prune back the clematis in a more or less random fashion, perhaps by as much as two-thirds, and to remove the offending stems by giving them a sharp tug. The final pruning can then be carried out at the correct time. The worst that can happen with such a strategy is that the clematis will start into growth in periods of mild weather. But the valuable basal buds will fortunately remain dormant.

Where species such as *Clematis tangutica* and *C. rehderiana* are used to cover unsightly objects, or are required simply to fill as large an area as possible, then they can be left unpruned. Over the years they will grow over and through themselves, providing a wonderful show of flowers and seed heads. But over the long term they will inevitably start to deteriorate as the proportion of old wood becomes greater than the new shoots which are able to bear the flowers.

At this stage it is beneficial to start rejuvenating the plants by pruning them back in easy stages over a period of two or three seasons. The plant will have produced a vigorous root system over the years, but it will still have difficulty producing shoots from very old and gnarled stems. So if you prune it back too hard, the resulting shoots will be somewhat weak and spindly, and will take many years to recover. By pruning back in easy stages you will allow the clematis to rejuvenate itself slowly, and you can still enjoy the flowers each year.

Clematis texensis *'Duchess of Albany'* requires hard pruning.

General maintenance

If you are going to obtain the best results from clematis and climbers, then you'll need to follow a general maintenance routine through the year. This really doesn't amount to much, but the little extra effort required will more than pay for itself in the final result.

Spring

As the days lengthen and the temperature rises, so all plants will start into growth. Many climbers, especially those trained against the house walls, will require pruning to keep them in bounds. The ivies and Virginia creepers can be clipped back hard, and removed from around windows and roof timbers. This will keep them tight against the wall and provide plenty of colourful new foliage. Clematis will also need to be pruned according to their particular needs, and retied to their supports.

At this time of the year, when the ground is moist and beginning to warm up, it's best to apply a dressing of a good general fertiliser, followed by a mulch of organic matter — either bark or compost. This will provide a sound foundation for new growth and also for flowers.

The weeds will also be starting to grow, and it's important to keep these under control.

Weeds can harbour a variety of pests, as well as competing for the available food and moisture. Using a hoe is not really advisable in the flower garden. Although a very effective tool, it can also cause a great deal of damage. Clematis and some other climbing plants form roots very near to the surface, and these can be badly damaged, as can the stems themselves, by too-diligent hoeing. It's far better to use a hand fork; versions of this are available with long handles, which are much easier to use.

Summer

During the summer months, when plants are in full growth, there is not very much that needs to be done.

The main requirement is to provide them with adequate food and water, and this is best done by means of liquid feeding. A high-potash feed such as tomato fertiliser, applied every couple of weeks with a can of water, and given to each clematis at least once a week, will keep your plants growing and flowering to their maximum potential.

The montana group of clematis may require some pruning. Wisteria grown against a wall will also benefit if you prune those shoots not required to increase the overall size of the plant; cut them back to about a foot (30 cm) in length in August. Other climbers may also have unwanted stems that should be cut back to keep them in bounds.

Apart from that, and an occasional spray against aphids, there is little that needs to be done except sit back and enjoy the fruits of your labours.

Autumn

As the temperatures drop, the plants start to become dormant and shed their leaves. Now's the time to stop feeding your plants and prepare them for the winter.

The most important task at this time of the year, as far as climbers are concerned, is to ensure that they are securely tied to their supports. Old ties should also be inspected to see if they are cutting into the plants' stems, and if necessary replaced using soft twine. The smaller shoots can be tied in using paper-covered wire ties.

Seed from clematis can also be gathered and sown immediately. They don't need protection from frost, which they actually need for germination, but they do have to be shielded from the attentions of mice and birds. A covering of chicken wire will normally do the trick.

Plants in containers should be continually checked to see if they have dried out. After a period of frost the compost can become very dry, and plants can succumb to drought even at this time of the year.

Winter

This is the time to plan for next year. But don't dig out the planting holes in preparation. If you do this, not only will you end up with a series of tiny ponds, but the soil will become cold. If you leave digging to the moment of planting, then the soil will still be warm.

Wisterias can be given their final prune, cutting back those stems pruned in August to an inch or two (a few centimetres) from the main shoot. The later-flowering clematis can also be tidied up in preparation for their final pruning in February or March.

Tying in a climbing rose

Pests and diseases

Animal pests

Climbers are not particularly prone to attack from the variety of wildlife that can wreak havoc with other less robust plants. In general they are remarkably resistant, and the amount of growth they produce in a season soon covers up the odd nibbled leaf. The climbing roses are of course prone to the same problems as their non-climbing relatives, and can therefore be dealt with in a similar fashion.

Earwigs may be lovable-looking creatures, but they are rather too partial to clematis. The flowers in the picture bear the scars of their greed.

The list that follows is designed to help you isolate potential problems. It should not put you off growing these wonderful plants.

Aphids

This is the name given to the group of pests that includes the well-known greenfly and blackfly, which attack nearly every plant at some time during the growing season.

They suck the sap from the young shoots, and cause stems and leaves to curl, generally in a downward direction. They also exude a sticky residue that is much loved by ants, which are often seen moving up and down a badly infected plant. In severe cases a black mould forms over the surface of the leaves.

Gardeners are often confused by the mass of white specks which appear during an aphid attack. They sometimes mistake these for whitefly, when in fact they are the husks of dead aphids.

Aphids can be controlled by a vast array of chemicals, many of which only kill off the aphids, leaving the beneficial lacewings, ladybirds and hover-flies to carry on their own form of pest control.

Earwigs

These rather lovable creatures are responsible for chewing chunks out of leaves and flowers, especially those of clematis, to which they are very partial.

Earwigs are also rather difficult to control. For as they only venture out during the night, no amount of spraying will have the slightest effect. The various dusts that are

This honeysuckle has fallen victim to aphid attack. When treating such infestations, make sure you don't kill off the ladybirds, which being partial to aphids act as a natural pest control.

recommended for the purpose will simply make your plant look as though it has a terminal case of mildew.

There is a much simpler and more effective plan of attack. All you need to do is to place the skin of half a grapefruit at the base of the plant. The earwigs will return to spend the day underneath it, at which point both the grapefruit skin

and the earwigs can be disposed of together.

Froghoppers
These pests are responsible for the frothy mass known as cuckoo spit. This hides a small green insect, which sucks up sap and in severe cases can severely stunt the growth of the plant.

Froghoppers can simply be washed away with a forceful stream of water from your sprayer before they can do any damage.

Scale insects
Sometimes small brown scales appear on the leaf undersides of evergreen climbers (*Clema-*

tis armandii is especially prone). Also, as with aphid attacks, a black, sooty mould covers the leaves. The little beast involved is the scale insect. Under each brown hump lives a small bug, which sucks the sap from the plant.

Because scale insects colonise the underside of leaves, they often build up large colonies before you notice them. They are also rather difficult to control. Only repeated sprays of a good systemic insecticide in the early spring will have any effect. Mercifully, scale insects are not particularly common, and are more liable to appear on evergreens grown in a conservatory.

Slugs and snails
No section on pests would be complete without some mention of these two doyens of the plant-eating world. Slugs and snails do more damage to clematis than any other creature, with the possible exception of a gardener using a hoe. It's usually the slugs that devour the succulent basal shoots, while the snails' ability to climb gives them access to a hearty meal from the flowers.

There's a huge armoury of control methods available, but none so effective as placing a layer of sharp grit around the base of the plant. Slugs and snails hate this. What is more, you only have to do it once and the grit doesn't get washed away.

The cuckoo spit on this rose leaf conceals the presence of a froghopper, which must be flushed away immediately before it can damage the plant.

Fungal diseases

Provided you water and feed your plants correctly, and don't leaving any jagged shoots when pruning, and remove dead leaves and other debris on a regular basis, then you probably won't need to read this section.

Plants are living things, and diseases generally strike those which are weak and under-nourished — not those which have built up a strong immune system.

The diseases that follow are the ones most usually encountered. All of them can be controlled by cultivation methods and the occasional spraying.

Mice

These little rodents can do vast amounts of damage in winter, especially if you are growing clematis through heathers. The covering of heathers makes an ideal winter habitat for mice, and they don't have to go far for a meal.

Growing clematis through a clay drainpipe for the first foot will help to control this problem. But a cat is probably the best answer. Mouse traps are not a good idea. It's so easy to forget where you've set one in a bed of heathers, with dire results to your fingers when you start weeding the following spring.

Ants

Sometimes plants wilt and die for no apparent reason, particularly those planted at the base of a wall. Should this occur, it's always a good idea to check around the base of the plant for an ants' nest. These creatures make a vast complex of tunnels when creating their nests, and this sharpens the drainage so much that the climbers suffer from drought.

Ants can be easily dealt with by sprinkling an ant powder over the soil surface.

Clematis 'Yellow Queen' is such a martyr to clematis wilt that this cultivar is best avoided altogether.

Clematis wilt

This is the name that strikes terror in the heart of many gardeners. It first became a problem in the early part of the century, and ever since then discussions have raged as to what it is and how it can be controlled.

The symptoms are dramatic but not necessarily terminal. Wilt usually strikes just as the clematis is about to flower: the first signs are a slight greying of the leaves, followed by a total collapse of the plant (though sometimes only one shoot is affected) as though it

Clematis 'Marie Boisselot' **(above left)** *and C. 'Countess of Lovelace'* **(above)** *are both vulnerable to wilt, but respond well to treatment.*

has suddenly dried out. At this point many plants are consigned prematurely to the bonfire — which is a mistake, as they can often recover.

Clematis wilt is thought to be caused by a fungus, which attacks the plant at the point where the soil and air meet, blocking the flow of sap and thus causing the plant to wilt. It must be said that on many occasions the same symptoms

This plant shows signs of clematis wilt. The same symptoms may be caused by mechanical damage, but either way the treatment is the same.

soon the plant will be back to full vigour.

Certain clematis varieties seem to be more prone to wilt than others. These are the ones that have caused the most problems in the past:

● *C.* 'Countess of Lovelace'

● *C.* 'Moonlight'

● *C.* 'Duchess of Edinburgh'

● *C.* 'Marie Boisselot'

● *C.* 'Horn of Plenty'

Mildew

This disease strikes mainly those clematis growing in the shade, and where there is poor air circulation. It can be recognised from the white powdery markings on the leaves, which if it is left unchecked will eventually turn brown and die. The later-flowering varieties are also more prone to attack.

Mildew can be easily controlled by a preventative spray with a specific fungicide.

Grey mould

This fungus can be discerned from a light-grey fluffy growth that starts to form on dead leaves, usually in the autumn. If left untreated, the disease will spread rapidly to the living parts of the plant.

can be due to mechanical damage. One of the stems may have been cut by a hoe or damaged by the pet cat. Either way the treatment is the same.

Cut out and burn all the dead and dying shoots down to ground level, and give the plant a good soaking. Provided that you've planted it correctly and buried a few buds beneath the soil, the plant stands a good chance of recovery. Some precautions against slugs will allow shoots to come up from below ground level, and very

70

The best cure is prevention. Remove all dead material from around the plant. This fungus is also more prevalent on plants grown in a conservatory, where good ventilation will keep it at bay.

Other problems

Bottom leaves dying
This is perfectly normal. It will happen during the late summer period, particularly to the later-flowering varieties. As the plant grows it has no more use for these bottom leaves, so discards them to save energy for flowering.

Green flowers
The early-flowering hybrids are the most prone to this problem, which flower arrangers love to make use of. It is caused partly by the weather and partly by a lack of potash. A good feed with tomato fertiliser will soon rectify the problem.

No flowers
Sometimes for no reason a clematis will 'go blind' and fail to flower. High-potash fertilisers will help to alleviate the problem, as will pruning the shoots back by half, which will sometimes make the clematis produce flower buds later in the season.

A fine specimen of Rosa banksiae *'Lutescens' growing with* Ceanothus *'Concha'*

Climbers for flowers

Although it often seems like it, clematis are not the only climbing plants that give a glorious display of flowers and have lots of different uses at the same time.

There are many places where clematis may be the worst choice of plant. In hot, dry positions, for instance, where only copious amounts of water and large amounts of time will give clematis even half a chance, then plants such as abutilons and jasmines come into their own. Both these plants do especially well in full sun: the abutilons bear their strange flowers similar to Turk's cap, while the jasmines carry small, starry flowers in a variety of colours, producing one of the most lovely of perfumes on a warm summer's night.

A constantly wet, shady spot is ideal for the climbing hydrangea *(Hydrangea petio-laris)*, especially if you need it to cover a large area. Once established, this vigorous plant will quickly cover a large wall, and with its flat white clusters of flowers in June it looks

Left and **above:** Rosa *'Treasure Trove'*

superb growing up and through a tall tree. This is also one of the few flowering climbers that will adhere to its host by means of sticky pads, which tend to appear after a couple of seasons.

For their sheer profusion of flowers, and a scent that says everything there is to say about the British summer, you don't have to look further than the honeysuckle *(Lonicera* spp.).

their flowers under a thick canopy of foliage. The foliage is also somewhat liable to mildew, which is worse if the plant is growing in a dry situation. The best varieties for growing in shade unfortunately don't have any scent, but their flowers tend to be even more exotic, especially with *Lonicera tragophylla*.

For a really exotic, indeed almost tropical, effect why not try the passion flower (*Passiflora caerulea*). This very vigorous climber is perfectly hardy in all but the very coldest aspects. Given a sunny wall

Continued on page 76

The evergreen honeysuckle Lonicera tragophylla doesn't have much scent, but the flowers look wonderfully exotic.

The many forms of the common native honeysuckle (*L. periclymenum*) which are now available look superb when allowed to scramble over tree stumps, or up and over arches and pergolas. Hawk moths and bees also find these flowers irresistible, and the added sound of these insects going about their business can add yet another dimension to the garden.

Among the only drawbacks with honeysuckles are that the evergreen forms, although sweetly scented, tend to hide

A selection of flowering climbers

Species or cultivar	Description	Position	Flowering time	Growth height	Spread
Abutilon megapotamicum	yellow flowers with purple anthers	best on a warm wall	Jul.	3 ft (1 m)	3 ft (1 m)
A. m. 'Variegatum'	red/yellow flowers; yellow-mottled leaves	sunny, warm, well drained	Jul.	6 ft (2 m)	3 ft (1 m)
A. m. 'Wisley Red'	bell-shaped red flowers	sunny, well drained	Jul.	6 ft (2 m)	3 ft (1 m)
Akebia quinata	fragrant reddish-purple flowers; semi-evergreen leaves	sun or light shade	Apr.	9 ft (3 m)	
Aristolochia macrophylla (Dutchman's pipe)	purple-brown flowers	sunny, warm wall	Jun.	12 ft (3.5 m)	6 ft (2 m)
Billardiera longiflora	greenish-yellow flowers; bright-blue fruits later	sunny wall	Jun.–Jul.	6 ft (2 m)	3 ft (1 m)
Campsis radicans 'Flava' (trumpet vine)	rich-yellow flowers	sunny wall	late summer	15 ft (4.5 m)	6 ft (2 m)
C. × *tagliabuana* 'Mme Galen'	salmon-red flowers	sunny wall	late summer	15 ft (4.5 m)	6 ft (2 m)
Calystegia hederacea 'Flore Pleno'	shell-pink double flowers	sunny, well drained	summer	6 ft (2 m)	can be invasive
Eccremocarpus scaber	orange/scarlet flowers	well drained, south or west wall	Jun.–Oct.	5 ft (1.5 m)	6 ft (2 m)
E. scaber 'Aurea'	tubular yellow flowers	sunny, well drained	summer	6 ft (2m)	3 ft (1 m)
Fallopia baldschuanica (Russian vine)	frothy white flower panicles; growth very vigorous	any aspect	June	25 ft (7.5 m)	15 ft (4.5 m)
Hydrangea petiolaris (climbing hydrangea)	large white flowers	shady wall (self-clinging)	Jun.	15 ft (4.5 m)	15 ft (4.5 m)
Jasminum officinale	fragrant pure-white flowers	sunny	Jul.	9 ft (3 m)	6 ft (2 m)
J. o. 'Affine'	white flowers tinged with pink	sunny	Jun.–Sep.	9 ft (3 m)	3 ft (1 m)
J. o. 'Aureum'	variegated foliage suffused with bright golden-yellow	sunny	Jul.	15 ft (4.5 m)	9 ft (3 m)
J. o. 'Argenteo-variegatum'	white flowers over variegated foliage	sunny	Jul.	15 ft (4.5 m)	9 ft (3 m)

Species or cultivar	Description	Position	Flowering time	Growth height	Spread
Jasminum × stephanense	fragrant pale-pink flowers	warm, sunny wall	Jun.	20 ft (6 m)	12 ft (3.5 m)
Lonicera alseuosmoides	yellow-and-purple flowers; evergreen	sunny, well drained	Jul.–Sep.	9 ft (3 m)	3 ft (1 m)
L. × americana	long, very fragrant flowers with purple outers	sunny	Jul.	15 ft (4.5 m)	12 ft (3.5 m)
L. × brownii 'Dropmore Scarlet'	tubular scarlet flowers	sun or part shade	Jul.–Oct.	9 ft (3 m)	6 ft (2 m)
L. caprifolium 'Anne Fletcher'	large cream flowers, waxy and very fragrant	sunny	Jun.–Jul.	3 ft (1 m)	6 ft (2 m)
L. etrusca	large whorls of fragrant cream/yellow flowers	sunny	Jun.–Jul.	9 ft (3 m)	6 ft (2 m)
L. heckrotii 'Gold Flame'	orangy-yellow flowers	most aspects	Jul.–Aug.	12 ft (3.5 m)	6 ft (2 m)
L. henryi	yellow flowers stained red; evergreen	sun or shade	Jul.	12 ft (3.5 m)	9 ft (3 m)
L. japonica 'Aureo-reticulata'	golden-netted summer foliage	shaded, moist	Jun.	6 ft (2 m)	3 ft (1 m)
L. j. 'Halliana'	fragrant white flowers fading to yellow	sun or shade	Jun.–Jul.	15 ft (4.5 m)	9 ft (3 m)
L. j. 'Repens'	fragrant yellow flowers; red-flushed leaves less prone to mildew than others	sun/part shade	Jun.–Jul.	9 ft (3 m)	6 ft (2 m)
L. periclymenum 'Belgica' (early Dutch honeysuckle)	purple flowers with white tubes, very fragrant	sunny	May–Jun.	12 ft (3.5 m)	9 ft (3 m)
L. p. 'Graham Thomas'	very fragrant cream flowers	sunny	Jul.	9 ft (3 m)	6 ft (2 m)
L. p. 'Serotina' (late Dutch honeysuckle)	very fragrant purple flowers with white tubes	sunny	Jul.–Aug.	12 ft (3.5 m)	9 ft (3 m)
L. p. 'Red Gables'	fragrant cream/red flowers	sunny	Jul.	9 ft (3 m)	6 ft (2 m)
L. sulphurea	fragrant pale-yellow flowers	sunny	Jun.–Jul.	9 ft (3 m)	6 ft (2 m)
L. tellmanniana	bright-orange tubular flowers	shady	June	12 ft (3.5 m)	9 ft (3 m)

Species or cultivar	Description	Position	Flowering time	Growth height	Spread
Passiflora caerulea (passion flower)	curiously shaped white/purple flowers	sheltered, sunny wall	summer	15 ft (4.5 m)	6 ft (2 m)
P. c. 'Constance Elliot'	curiously shaped pure-white flowers	sunny wall	summer	12 ft (3.5 m)	9 ft (3 m)
Solanum crispum 'Glasnevin'	rich purple-blue flowers	warm, sunny wall	summer	15 ft (4.5 m)	9 ft (3 m)
S. jasminoides 'Album'	white flowers with yellow beaks	warm, sunny wall	summer	9 ft (3 m)	6 ft (2 m)
Trachelospermum asiaticum	fragrant buff-yellow flowers; evergreen	sunny wall	summer	9 ft (3 m)	3 ft (1 m)
T. jasminoides 'Variegatum'	evergreen leaves with creamy-white margins	sheltered, sunny wall	summer	9 ft (3 m)	3 ft (1 m)
Wisteria floribunda 'Burford'	huge racemes of scented violet-blue flowers	south or west wall	Jun.	20 ft (6 m)	12 ft (3.5 m)
W. f. 'Macrobotrys'	long racemes of blue-mauve flowers	sunny, warm wall	Jun.	15 ft (4.5 m)	9 ft (3 m)
W. × formosa 'Black Dragon'	racemes of purple double flowers	south or west wall	Jun.	12 ft (3.5 m)	12 ft (3.5 m)
W. sinensis	fragrant lilac flowers	sunny, south or west wall	May–Jun.	15 ft (4.5 m)	15 ft (4.5 m)
W. s. 'Alba'	short racemes of fragrant white flowers	sunny, south or west wall	May–Jun.	15 ft (4.5 m)	15 ft (4.5 m)

to grow on, it will produce masses of curiously formed purple-and-white flowers every year. Because of its vigour it needs to be pruned back quite hard each year, especially if it's growing in fertile soil.

This is a plant to starve if you want lots of flowers, but alas it is not the species which bears edible fruit. Passion fruits come from *P. edulis* — the granadilla — which requires the protection of a conservatory in order to produce anything worthwhile.

The main advantage of climbers is that they tend to occupy vertical rather than horizontal space. If more gardeners thought in these terms, then they would grow far more of the vigorous climbing roses. *Rosa filipes* 'Kiftsgate' and its companions are often avoided because of their undoubted vigour. Yet half a dozen of these varieties can been seen growing and flowering to perfection in a medium-sized garden. Such varieties include *R.* 'Frances E.

Lester' with flowers coloured like apple blossom, *R.* 'Treasure Trove' with its scented apricot blossoms, and the pure-white *R.* 'Niagara'. All three are an amazing sight cascading down like a multicoloured waterfall through a variety of mature trees, some of them 50 ft (9 m) in height.

Left, **below left** and **below:** Rosa *'Frances E. Lester'*

Climbers for foliage

These are plants which are grown primarily for the beauty and effectiveness of their foliage.

The most common foliage climber in Britain is the common ivy (*Hedera helix*), which can be seen covering banks and climbing up trees wherever it is allowed. The cultivated forms are equally useful for the same purpose. Being hardy and vigorous, they will grow in the most difficult of situations, even in deep shade on dry soils.

Ivy climbs by means of sticky pads which adhere to walls and other plants, and this has led to the misconception that ivy kills trees and damages buildings. Where buildings are concerned, this is only true if the pointing and general fabric is in poor condition in the first place. And the only harm ivy will do to a tree is to provide extra wind resistance, which if the tree has passed maturity can prove its final downfall. The pads are merely to help the plant climb, and don't rob the host plant of any nourishment. In some cases ivy has even been shown to protect buildings and trees from damp and decay.

Ivy benefits from being given quite a severe haircut every spring. Clipping back old leaves and any straggling shoots will stimulate it into producing masses of attractive new growth, and will also keep it tight back against either the wall or the host plant.

One final plea must be made on behalf of this much-maligned plant — it is a wonderful plant for wildlife. The

Below: Hedera helix *'Cristata' is seen to best advantage in the snow.*

Below right: *The golden hop (Humulus lupulus 'Aurea') can grow as high as 20 ft (6 m) in a single season, but dies back to the ground every winter.*

A selection of climbers for foliage effect

Species or cultivar	Description	Position	Growth height	Spread
Ampelopsis brevi-pedunculata 'Elegans'	leaves mottled white and pink; treat as scrambler	sheltered		
Celastrus scandens	orange fruits with scarlet seeds	sun or shade	20 ft (6 m)	12 ft (3.5 m)
Cissus striata	dark-green leaves; red/purple fruits; evergreen	warm, sunny wall	20 ft (6 m)	12 ft (3.5 m)
Hedera colchica (Persian ivy)	large, deep-green leaves; evergreen	shady	15 ft (4.5 m)	9 ft (3 m)
H. c. 'Paddy's Pride'	large, oval, yellow-edged leaves; evergreen	sun or light shade	9 ft (3 m)	9 ft (3 m)
H. c. 'Dentata Variegata'	green/grey leaves with cream margins	partial shade	9 ft (3 m)	9 ft (3 m)
H. helix 'Salt and Pepper'	young foliage mottled pink and cream	sun or shade	15 ft (4.5 m)	9 ft (3 m)
H. h. 'Buttercup'	young foliage suffused with yellow; not a strong grower	sunny	9 ft (3 m)	9 ft (3 m)
H. h. 'Marginata'	silver-margined leaves; evergreen	sun or light shade	9 ft (3 m)	6 ft (2 m)
H. h. 'Cavendishii'	cream-margined leaves; evergreen	sun or shade	15 ft (4.5 m)	12 ft (3.5 m)
H. h. 'Sagittifolia'	narrow, green leaves; evergreen	sun or shade	15 ft (4.5 m)	12 ft (3.5 m)
H. h. 'Cristata'	young leaves crinkled and bright green; wonderful in winter	sun or shade	12 ft (3.5 m)	6 ft (2 m)
Humulus lupulus 'Aureus' (golden hop)	golden foliage in summer	sunny	15 ft (4.5 m)	6 ft (2 m)
Parthenocissus henryana	silver-veined leaves with superb autumn colour	any aspect	15 ft (4.5 m)	6 ft (2 m)
P. quinquefolia (Virginia creeper)	green leaves with brilliant autumn colour	any aspect	20 ft (6 m)	15 ft (4.5 m)
P. tricuspidata 'Veitchii' (Boston Ivy)	brilliant autumn colour; can be trimmed	sun or shade (self-clinging)	15 ft (4.5 m)	20 ft (6 m)
Vitis 'Brant'	sweet, aromatic grapes; good autumn leaf colour; prune annually	sunny, warm wall	25 ft (7.7 m)	10 ft (3 m)
V. coignetiae	large, heart-shaped leaves; fiery autumn colour	sun or shade	20 ft (6 m)	12 ft (3.5 m)
V. vinifera 'Purpurea'	deep-purple leaves in summer; small black grapes	sunny, warm wall	12 ft (3.5 m)	9 ft (3 m)

Clematis in pots

leaves, being evergreen, provide marvellous winter quarters for a variety of bird and insect species. The flowers are also rich in nectar, and the berries that follow are a valuable food source.

Another valuable source of food and drink, but this time for humans, is the grape vine (*Vitis* spp.). Two varieties in particular provide decorative foliage and reasonable crops of fruit. *Vitis* 'Brant' produces black grapes in abundance — superb for wine making and not bad as a dessert fruit. Soft-green foliage throughout the summer turns a fiery scarlet with the approach of autumn before finally falling. *V. vinifera* 'Purpurea' also produces black grapes — albeit not as large as *V.* 'Brant' — but as the foliage matures during the summer it turns a deep purple, lightening again in autumn.

Both these vines require a sunny position to give of their best. They climb by means of tendrils, so some support will be necessary.

For golden foliage you can't beat the golden hop *(Humulus lupulus* 'Aurea'). This plant attaches itself to its host plant by twisting its stems around it as it makes its way skywards. It can manage 20 ft (6 m) in a season before dying down to ground level each year. Whether in sun or partial shade, its bright-golden leaves are superb if allowed to ramble through other plants, or up and through small trees.

Growing plants in pots and containers is a method of gardening that has become increasingly popular in recent years. This is partly because modern gardens tend to be much smaller, but also because nowadays there are so many different types and styles of container available, which means gardeners can be increasingly creative and adventurous in their choice of plant.

The choice of clematis depends on the manner of growth. Vigorous species such as *Clematis montana* will soon outgrow even the largest pot, becoming starved and bedraggled after a couple of seasons.

Clematis *'Mrs N. Thompson'* makes an excellent pot plant.

Some of the more vigorous hybrids will also run out of steam fairly quickly.

Clematis require a cool, moist root run, and growing one in a free-standing container inevitably opens the root system to the vagaries of the weather. In the summer the pot and its contents may become very hot and dry. In the winter, if it is not given some protection, the root system can be frozen solid. Both these extremes can result in the plant dying unless precautions are taken.

The choice of container is therefore an important issue. The most pleasing pots to look at are those made from traditional clay. These used to be regarded as expensive, but nowadays there are many

Clematis 'Bees Jubilee' in a pot

imported types that are excellent value, even if they lack the true character of the traditional hand-thrown pot.

Clay pots are porous, and as the water seeps through the pores it evaporates, keeping the roots of the plants cool. However, this can also mean the pot is liable to cracking in frosty weather. If size prevents you from taking your pots indoors for the winter, then it's advisable to wrap some kind of insulation around them to protect both the pot and the roots from the cold.

Plastic is much more robust than clay, but as there is no evaporation the roots can become very hot. Plastic pots can also become waterlogged unless there are plenty of drainage holes at the base. If you bear these points in mind, however, your plants will grow very happily in plastic pots. They are also light, which means they can be moved around more easily.

The size of the container is important if your clematis is to thrive for any length of time. You are not recommended to use a pot any smaller than 18 in (50 cm) in diameter. This size will give the plant adequate room to grow and develop over a number of years, and will also hold suffi-

cient water and nutrients to cope with its demands. Each year, when you prune the plant, you should carefully scrape off the top inch (2–3 cm) of soil and replace it with some fresh compost. If you do this, your clematis will grow and provide an abundance of flowers for many years.

The next important decision is the best compost to use. Remember that clematis like a good rich soil with lots of nutrients. A John Innes-type compost is always the best for this purpose. This formulation, developed many years ago, includes loam, which provides a good reservoir of nutrients and also retains adequate water without becoming too wet. Loam is also heavy, which helps prevent the container and its contents from blowing over in the wind.

Planting in a container is much the same as planting a clematis in the open ground. It's a good idea to plant fairly deep so as to cover up some of the basal buds, and to firm it in gently around the roots with your clenched fists. Finish the process with a good watering, allowing any excess water to drain away.

Once your clematis has become established, start feeding it with a good, well-balanced liquid feed — preferably one that is high in potash. Feed it at least once a week during the growing season. If you give too much feed, then salts can build up in the compost. So it's a good idea to miss one weekly feed each month, just watering normally to flush the compost through.

Suggested clematis varieties for growing in containers

All the varieties listed in the table below are suitable for growing in pots. However, some such as the alpinas and

A selection of clematis varieties for containers

Cultivar	Flowers	Position	Pruning needed	Flowering time
C. alpina 'Burford White'	small, white, bell-shaped	any aspect	none	Apr.–May
C. a. 'Columbine'	small, blue, bell-shaped	any aspect	none	Apr.
C. a. 'Constance'	ruby-red, bell-shaped	any aspect	none	Apr.
C. macropetala 'Maidwell Hall'	large, double, deep blue, bell-shaped	any aspect	none	Apr.–May
C. m. 'Markhams Pink'	small, pink	any aspect	none	Apr.–May
C. m. 'Orchid'	double, ruby-red with cream centre	any aspect	none	Apr.–May
C. 'Bees Jubilee'	large, deep pink with rose bar	shady	light	May–Jun.; Aug.
C. 'Carnaby'	medium, deep pink with deeper bar	shady	light	May–June
C. 'Comtesse de Bouchaud'	large, mauve-pink	any aspect	hard	Jul.–Aug.
C. 'Dawn'	large, pearly-pink	shady	light	May–Jun.; Aug.
C. 'Dr Ruppel'	large, pink with deeper bar	shady	light	May–Jul.
C. 'Duchess of Edinburgh'	medium, double, white	sunny	light	Jun.–Aug.
C. 'Duchess of Sutherland'	large, carmine	any aspect	light	Jun.–Aug.
C. 'Edith'	medium, white	any aspect	light	May–Sep.
C. 'Fireworks'	violet-mauve with carmine bar	any aspect	light	Jun.–Aug.
C. 'Lady Northcliffe'	medium, wedgwood blue	any aspect	light	Jun.–Aug.
C. 'Mrs N. Thompson'	large, blue with petunia bar	any aspect	light	Jun.–Aug.
C. 'Mrs P. B. Truax'	medium, periwinkle-blue	any aspect	light	May–Jun.
C. 'Royalty'	plum-purple, semi-double in May, single in late summer	any aspect	light	May–Aug.
C. 'Wadas Primrose'	large creamy-white	ideal for shade	light	May–Jun.

macropetalas have a short flowering period, so are probably not the best choice for free-standing displays in a conspicuous position.

Given a container of adequate size, you can also plant two varieties together such as *Clematis* 'Comtesse de Bouchaud' and *C.* 'Lady Northcliffe', which will provide an eye-catching display of flowers over a long period. Low-growing annuals can also be planted to provide colour at the base, and a degree of shade for the clematis roots.

Above: Clematis *'Duchess of Sutherland' is a double cultivar that produces single flowers later in the season.*

Clematis *'Fireworks' — an unusual cultivar that also goes well in a pot*

Using clematis as a cut flower

Considering that so many gardens, whatever their size, can boast at least one clematis plant, their value as a cut flower is often overlooked. If a clematis is well grown and flowering as it should, then there are immense possibilities for using the blooms on a lavish scale for producing floral decorations.

Clematis viticella 'Abundance' is a good candidate for flower arrangements.

Some practical points need to be made, however. When you are cutting flowers for arrangements, try to leave a little of the old wood attached, as this helps to keep the flowers from flagging prematurely. Cut the flowers the day before arranging them, and leave them overnight in plunged up to their necks in water. Use a bucket with a piece of rigid plastic net across the top to keep the blooms supported and stop them becoming watermarked.

Because of their natural growth habit, many of the smaller-flowered varieties have sprays of blooms arranged in pairs along their stems. Very conveniently, these flowers usually face in one direction, making them ideal for arrangements on stands, or in vases placed high up so that the sprays can trail. With arrangements of this type, the stems must be very firmly anchored into wet oasis. It's also worth considering whether you need to add some extra weight to the container to stop it over-balancing. The stems are also very effective if arranged along a shelf or windowsill.

When using larger-flowered varieties, it is more effective to

Clematis varieties suitable for cutting

Cultivar	Flowers	Position	Pruning needed	Flowering time	Growth height
C. 'Barbara Jackman'	large, blue with petunia bar	light shade	light	May–Jun.	10 ft (3 m)
C. 'Beauty of Worcester'	large, double, deep blue	sunny	light	May–Jul.	10 ft (3 m)
C. 'Carnaby'	medium, deep pink	shady	light	May–Jun.	6 ft (2 m)
C. 'Comtesse de Bouchaud'	large, mauve-pink	any aspect	hard	Jul.–Aug.	10 ft (3 m)
C. 'Daniel Deronda'	large, double, purple/blue	sunny	light	May–Aug.	10 ft (3 m)
C. 'Dawn'	large, pearly-pink	shady	light	May–Jun.; Aug.	10 ft (3 m)
C. 'Dr Ruppel'	large pink with deeper bar	shady	light	May–Jul.	10 ft (3 m)
C. 'Duchess of Edinburgh'	medium, double, white	sunny	light	Jun.–Aug.	10 ft (3 m)
C. 'Elsa Späth'	large, mid-blue	any aspect	light	May–Sep.	8 ft (2.5 m)
C. 'General Sikorsky'	large, mid-blue	any aspect	light	Jun.–Jul.	10 ft (3 m)
C. 'Gillian Blades'	large, white with faint mauve edge	any aspect	light	May–Jun.; Sep.	12 ft (3.5 m)
C. 'Gypsy Queen'	large, violet/purple	sunny	hard	Jul.–Aug.	12 ft (3.5 m)
C. 'H. F. Young'	large, wedgwood blue	any aspect	light	May–Jun.	10 ft (3 m)
C. 'Hagley Hybrid'	medium, rosy/mauve	any aspect	hard	Jun.–Aug.	8 ft (2.5 m)
C. 'Marie Boisselot'	large, white	any aspect	light	Jun.–Sep.	10 ft (3 m)
C. 'Pope John Paul II'	large, creamy-white with red centre	any aspect	light	May–Jun.; Sep.	8–12 ft (2.5–3.5 m)
C. 'Prince Charles'	medium, blue	any aspect	hard	Jun.–Sep.	10 ft (3 m)
C. 'Prins Hendrick'	large, blue	sunny	hard	Jul.–Aug.	10 ft (3 m)
C. 'The President'	large, rich purple	any aspect	light	May–Sep.	10 ft (3 m)
C. viticella 'Abundance'	small, red	any aspect	hard	Jul.–Sep.	12 ft (3.5 m)
C. v. 'Alba Luxurians'	small, creamy-white	any aspect	hard	Jul.–Sep.	10 ft (3 m)
C. v. 'Minuet'	small, white with mauve edge	any aspect	hard	Jul.–Aug.	12 ft (3.5 m)
C. v. 'Purpurea Plena Elegans'	small, double, purple	any aspect	hard	Jul.–Sep.	12 ft (3.5 m)
C. v. 'Royal Velours'	small, deep purple	any aspect	hard	Jul.–Sep.	12 ft (3.5 m)

cut individual stems and arrange the flowers singly. These can be used in mixed-flower arrangements or on their own with decorative foliage. Silver and grey leaves such as those of eucalyptus or *Artemisia* will make an excellent foil for the more purple-toned colours.

Even as late in the year as Christmas, clematis can have their uses in flower arrangements. Many late-flowering species such as *Clematis tangutica*, *C. vitalba* or *C. flammula*, and some of the large-flowered varieties, have silky seed heads. If you collect these before the weather damages them, they will last for long periods as part of a dry arrangement. If you gather them on their long stems before these become too brittle, then by winding medium-strength florist's wire around the stems you can make them both flexible and resilient, which will mean they are even more useful in mixed arrangements.

Above: Clematis *'Elsa Späth'*.

Below: *The rich-purple blooms of* Clematis *'The President' are seen here growing up bean poles. This cultivar can also be used as a cut flower.*

Above: Clematis *'Hagley Hybrid'*

Seed heads on their own may not look so good, but they can be very effective as part of a mixed flower arrangement.

Growing clematis and climbers in a conservatory

Over the past few years conservatories have become increasingly popular. Their primary purpose is to provide an extra room for the house, but they have the added advantage of augmenting the garden as well.

Many plants are too tender to grow outside but will thrive under the protection of a conservatory. There are others that will flourish outside but which indoors will flower either more prolifically or earlier in the year, lighting up the dark days of winter with a welcome splash of colour.

In general, clematis don't appreciate being grown indoors, preferring the cooler, more airy conditions outside. But there are some that will grow better in a conservatory.

The evergreen *Clematis cirrhosa* will not flower suc-

Right: Clematis florida *'Alba Plena'* will flower for much longer in a conservatory.

Below: Clematis *'Lady Northcliffe'* may be reluctant to flower out of doors, and benefits from the extra warmth of a conservatory.

Clematis for conservatories

Species or cultivar	Flowers	Flowering time	Growth height
C. armandii 'Snowdrift'	white, larger than on the species	Feb.	15 ft (4.5 m)
C. armandii 'Apple Blossom'	small, white, pink in bud.	Feb.	15 ft (4.5 m)
C. australis	small, creamy-yellow	Apr.–May	8 ft (2.5 m)
C. afoliata	small, creamy-yellow	Mar.–Apr.	10 ft (3 m)
C. cirrhosa	small, cream, speckled brown	Jan.–Mar.	20 ft (6 m)
C. c. balearica	small, cream, speckled	Jan.–Mar.	20 ft (6 m)
C. c. 'Freckles'	small, cream, red inside	Jan.–Mar.	20 ft (6 m)
C. c. 'Wisley Cream'	small, cream	Jan.–Mar.	20 ft (6 m)
C. 'Comtesse de Bouchaud'	large, mauve-pink	Jul.–Aug.	10 ft (3 m)
C. 'Dawn'	large, pearly-pink	May–Jun.; Aug.	10 ft (3 m)
C. 'Fair Rosamund'	large, white with pink bar, scented	May–Jun.	12 ft (3.5 m)
C. florida 'Alba Plena'	medium, greeny-white	Jun.–Sep.	8 ft (2.5 m)
C. florida 'Sieboldii'	medium, white with purple centre	Jun.–Sep.	8 ft (2.5 m)
C. forsteri	small, creamy-yellow, very fragrant	Apr.–May	10 ft (3 m)
C. 'H. F. Young'	large, wedgwood blue	May–Jun.	10 ft (3 m)

cessfully in northern counties, but given a position under cover it will bear masses of its creamy bell-like flowers from January onwards. *C. florida* 'Alba Plena' from China, and its relative *C. f.* 'Sieboldii', are both quite hardy, but in a conservatory they will provide a never-ending succession of their strange double flowers right up until Christmas. Some of the large-flowered hybrids will also flower more readily indoors. *Clematis* 'Lady Northcliffe', for example, tends not to flower in the north, but does so happily with the extra warmth that a conservatory affords. Other hybrids will flower much earlier, but these should be chosen carefully: often they will grow vigorously, lose their bottom leaves and produce only a few small flowers.

Other climbers that can be grown to good effect include the various forms of passion flower (if space permits) and abutilon, although these do tend to be rather badly affected by whitefly.

Climbers for conservatories

Species or cultivar	Description	Growth height	Spread
Abutilon megapotamicum	yellow flowers with purple anthers	3 ft (1 m)	3 ft (1 m)
A. m. 'Variegatum'	red/yellow flowers; leaves mottled yellow	6 ft (2 m)	3 ft (1 m)
A. m. 'Wisley Red'	bell-shaped red flowers	6 ft (2 m)	3 ft (1 m)
Lapageria rosea	large pink tubular flowers in late summer	8 ft (2.5 m)	4 ft (1 m)
Passiflora 'Eugene' (passion flower)	violet-and-white flowers in profusion	10 ft (3 m)	10 ft (3 m)
P. caerulea 'Constance Elliot'	pure-white passion flower	10 ft (3 m)	10 ft (3 m)

Scented clematis and climbers

To have a colourful garden is one thing, but the added pleasure of scented plants adds another even more pleasing aspect. Scents and perfumes are often remembered long after the vision of a garden has been forgotten.

The best-known scented plants are undoubtedly roses — particularly the more old-fashioned varieties such as the Pemberton Musks — and there are lots of superb climbing varieties to choose from. *Rosa* 'Kathleen Harrop' and *R.* 'Zephirine Drouhin' are both thornless with flowers in varying shades of pink. Thanks to their Bourbon parentage both of them have a wonderful perfume. They are also excellent hosts for clematis, as their lack of thorns makes the pruning of both plants much less painful.

Rosa 'Mme Alfred Carrière' is the classic rose for growing over and around a cottage door. It too is almost thornless (perhaps the reason it was originally chosen), and its white, slightly pink-flushed flowers have an exquisite perfume. This rose is also a wonderful host for clematis; it is seldom out of bloom, and blue clematis varieties such as *Clematis* 'Lady Northcliffe' give the rose just that little bit of extra sparkle.

Clematis in general are not among the most highly scented of plants. There is only one of the large-flowered hybrids that can make such a claim. *Clematis* 'Fair Rosamund' is supposed to have the scent of wild violets, but this may be more a case of wishful thinking than of hard fact. Some of the species, notably *C. flammula*, and varieties such as *C.* × *triternata* 'Rubro-Marginata', have a very good perfume that also wafts in the air. On a warm summer's evening, a single

Wisteria floribunda *'Burford'* is not only wonderful to look at — it has a wonderful fragrance too.

*Our native honeysuckle (*Lonicera periclymenum*) and its cultivars have always been noted for their beautiful scent. L. p. 'Graham Thomas' is the variety shown here.*

specimen of *C. flammula* can fill the garden with a delicious vanilla aroma. The herbaceous *C. recta* exudes a sweet honey scent that attracts vast numbers of insects, especially butterflies and the beneficial hoverflies, whose larvae devour huge quantities of greenfly. This species and its varieties grow to only 3 ft (1 m) in height, but can spread out to about the same width.

Rosa brunonii 'La Mortola' has a pleasantly musky scent.

Of all the scented climbers, by far the best and the most reliable is the honeysuckle (*Lonicera* spp.). The many varieties of our common native honeysuckle *L. periclymenum* take a lot of beating. Given a good sunny position, they will fill the garden with the scents of a traditional English summer. Probably the most highly scented of all the honeysuckles is *L. × americana*. A cross between the European

species *L. caprifolium* and *L. etrusca*, it provides a spectacular show of flowers in mid-summer, and the wonderful perfume is fully airborne.

Clematis *'Lady Northcliffe'* will give a fragrant rose just that little bit of extra sparkle.

Clematis for scent

Species or cultivar	Flowers	Position	Pruning needed	Flowering time	Growth height
Clematis armandii	small, white, scented	sheltered	none	Mar.–Apr.	30 ft (9 m)
C. a. 'Apple Blossom'	small, white, pink in bud, very fragrant	sheltered	none	Mar.–Apr.	30 ft (9 m)
C. a. 'Snowdrift'	larger than species, white, very fragrant	sheltered	none	Mar.–Apr.	15 ft (4.5 m)
C. 'Fair Rosamund'	large, white with light-pink bar, faint perfume of violets	any aspect	light	May–Jun.	12 ft (3.5 m)
C. flammula	small, white; wonderful airborne scent of vanilla	any position	hard	Aug.–Oct.	12 ft (3.5 m)
C. heracleifolia 'Wyevale'	small, deep blue (herbaceous)	any aspect	hard	Aug.–Oct.	3 ft (1 m)
C. montana	small, white, in profusion	any aspect	none	Apr.–May	30 ft (9 m)
C. m. 'Elizabeth'	small, soft pink	any aspect	none	May–Jun.	30 ft (9 m)
C. m. 'Pink Perfection'	small, pink, scented	any aspect	none	May	30 ft (9 m)
C. recta	small, white (herbaceous)	any aspect	hard	May–Jun.	3 ft (1 m)
C. recta 'Purpurea'	small, white (herbaceous)	any aspect	hard	May–Jun.	3 ft (1 m)
C. rehderiana	small, yellow; scent of cowslips	any aspect	hard	Sep.–Oct.	20 ft (6 m)
C. × triternata 'Rubro-Marginata'	small, white with violet edges	any aspect	hard	Aug.–Sep.	20 ft (6 m)

A selection of fragrant climbers

Species or cultivar	Description	Position	Flowering time	Growth height	Spread
Akebia quinata	fragrant reddish-purple flowers	sun or light shade	late spring	10 ft (3 m)	6 ft (2 m)
Jasminum officinale	fragrant pure-white flowers	sunny	Jul.	10 ft (3 m)	12 ft (3.5 m)
J. o. 'Affine'	white flowers tinged with pink	best sunny	Jun.; Sep.	10 ft (3 m)	3 ft (1 m)
J. × *stephanense*	fragrant pale-pink flowers	warm, sunny wall	Jun.–Jul.	20 ft (6 m)	12 ft (3.5 m)
Lonicera × *americana*	long fragrant purple flowers with cream inner tubes	sunny	Jul.	20 ft (6 m)	12 ft (3.5 m)
L. caprifolium 'Anne Fletcher'	large cream flowers, waxy and very fragrant	sunny for best scent	summer	3 ft (1 m)	12 ft (3.5 m)
L. japonica 'Halliana'	fragrant white flowers fading to yellow; evergreen	sun or shade (prone to mildew)	Jun.–Jul.	15 ft (4.5 m)	10 ft (3 m)
L. periclymenum 'Belgica' (early Dutch honeysuckle)	very fragrant purple flowers with white inner tubes	sunny	summer	12 ft (2.5 m)	10 ft (3 m)
L. p. 'Serotina' (late Dutch honeysuckle)	highly scented purple flowers with white inner tubes	sunny	summer	12 ft (2.5 m)	10 ft (3 m)
L. p. 'Graham Thomas'	very fragrant cream-coloured flowers	sunny	Jul.–Aug.	10 ft (3 m)	12 ft (3.5 m)
Trachelospermum jasminoides	very fragrant small white flowers; glossy-green leaves; evergreen	sheltered, sunny wall	summer	10 ft (3 m)	3 ft (1 m)
Wisteria floribunda 'Burford'	in huge racemes of highly scented lilac-blue flowers	south or west wall	spring	30 ft (9 m)	12 ft (3.5 m)
W. f. 'Macrobotrys'	long racemes of blue/mauve flowers	sunny, warm wall	early spring	10 ft (3 m)	10 ft (3 m)
W. f. 'Premature'	racemes of very fragrant mauve/purple flowers	south or west wall	Jun.	12 ft (3.5 m)	12 ft (3.5 m)
W. f. 'Alba'	long racemes of white flowers tinged with mauve	sunny; south or west	Jun.	30 ft (9 m)	15 ft (4.5 m)
W. sinensis	fragrant lilac-coloured flowers	sunny; south or west	May–Jun.	30 ft (9 m)	30 ft (9 m)

Where to see the plants displayed

One of the gardener's greatest pleasures in life is to visit other gardens and see how other gardeners use plants. Nowadays there is a huge amount of choice available, from the small private garden to the majestic estates surrounding this country's great stately homes. All are worth a visit, and it would be surprising if you failed to see at least one clematis in even the smallest of them.

Probably the most famous clematis garden is the one at Burford near Tenbury Wells on the Shropshire–Worcestershire border, which for nearly 40 years was the home of the late John Treasure. This garden, which holds the National Clematis Collection, has clematis growing up trees, through bushes and over walls — in fact, anywhere a clematis will grow, there will be one. A perfectionist by nature, John Treasure's skill and artistry has rarely been matched. He trained clematis to mingle in a natural way with other plants, either complementing them in colourful associations, or growing seemingly at random amongst their hosts. Few people realised the painstaking care and thought that went into the placing of every stem: each one was carefully pegged down or tied to give maximum effect. Today the gardens are still open and continue to thrive. They are very much worth a visit, both to see the collection and to gather ideas for your own garden.

Another great garden is Great Dixter in Sussex, whose clematis are well known from the writings of its owner Christopher Lloyd, a longtime friend of John Treasure. The two initially collaborated in setting up the Treasures of Tenbury nurseries (see panel), and together they were probably more responsible than anyone else for making clematis as popular as they are today.

The various gardens open in aid of charities, in particular those featured in the Yellow Book, are always worth a visit. At these gardens there is always the chance to talk to the owners and swap information

Specialist nurseries

Beamish Clematis Nursery
Burntwood Cottage
Stoney Lane
Beamish
Co. Durham, DH9 0SJ
Tel. 019137 00202

Caddicks Clematis Nursery
Lymm Road
Thelwall
Warrington, WA4 2TG
Tel. 01925 757196

The Clematis Centre
Woodcote Park Nursery
Ripley Road
Send
Woking, Surrey
Tel. 01483 223623

Taylor's Nursery
Sutton Road
Sutton, Nr Askern
Doncaster
S. Yorks, DN6 9JZ
Tel. 01302 700716

Great Dixter Nurseries
Northiam
Rye
East Sussex, TN31 6PH
Tel. 01797 253107

Robin Savill
The Clematis Specialist
2 Bury Cottages
Bury Road, Pleshey
Chelmsford,
Essex, CM3 1HB
Tel. 01245 237380

Thorncroft Clematis Nursery
The Lings
Reymerston
Norwich
Norfolk, NR9 4QG
Tel. 01953 850407

Treasures of Tenbury Ltd
Tenbury Wells
Hereford & Worcester
WR15 8HQ
Tel. 01584 810777

A full list of clematis nurseries can be obtained from the British Clematis Society at the address opposite.

The British Clematis Society

— and often there are choice plants for sale that are rarely available elsewhere.

The many gardening shows that are now staged are also useful places for seeing new varieties and evaluating their potential. It is here that you will be able to see the varieties offered by the specialist nurseries. These small businesses provide a much wider range of clematis than you will usually find in your local garden centre, and most of them offer a mail-order service.

A selection of specialist nurseries is given in the panel.

The most famous clematis garden is the one at Burford House on the Shropshire–Herefordshire border. It is also home to many other lovely climbers, as this wisteria-covered portico shows.

The British Clematis Society was formed in 1991, and has shown a dramatic growth in membership. Its aims are to impart a greater knowledge of clematis to gardeners, and to provide a platform where like-minded enthusiasts can share their experiences — and indeed, it does just that.

For just a few pounds a year there are an enormous number of benefits that members can enjoy. The annual journal is one of the most informative and best-produced of its kind. Full of helpful tips and information, it caters very cleverly for both the beginner and the experienced grower, rivalling many of the more famous and expensive society journals. Supplements are issued, keeping you up to date with new introductions. The list of events is very comprehensive,

ranging from a stand at the Malvern Spring Show to visits to nurseries and gardens that are not normally open to the general public.

Plant sales are organised at the society's meetings and, together with the annual seed exchange, offer the chance to obtain something new and exciting. There is also a slide library, and advice on all aspects of clematis culture is freely given to members.

Details of membership are available from:

The Membership Secretary
British Clematis Society
Mr A. S. Heywood-Jones
Lock Waters
Wargrave Road
Henley-on-Thames
Oxon RG9 3HX
Tel. 01491 412789

Clematis 'Royalty'

Index